Castrol Motorcycle Racing Manual

Edited by Mike Nicks
with contributions from 10
top experts in road racing

PSL

Patrick Stephens, London

First published - April 1973

ISBN 0 85059 122 8.

Text set in 9 on 10pt Times Roman. Printed in Great Britain on Brochure Printing 118gm² for Patrick Stephens Limited, 9 Ely Place, London EC1N 6SQ, by Blackfriars Press Limited, Leicester LE5 4BS. Bound by Hunter & Foulis Limited, Edinburgh EH7 4NP.

Contents

Editor's introduction

MOTOR RACING enthusiasts are encouraged in their hobby by a large and varied selection of books on the sport. But even today, motorcyclists are offered only a limited range of publications to supplement the weekly and monthly newspapers and magazines. I am sure that this new venture by Castrol and Patrick Stephens Ltd will help to fill that gap.

Some of the most respected names in road racing have contributed chapters to the *Castrol Motorcycle Racing Manual*. Photographs—a vital addition to a book which covers such a colourful sport as road racing—have been provided by three of the country's top experts in this field, Nick Nicholls, Malcolm Carling and Brian Holder.

The combination of all these talents adds up to an informative and topical commentary on road racing today. I hope that the experienced competitor and the knowledgeable spectator will gain as much from these pages as the newcomer to a sport which is now enjoying what the Japanese would call another 'golden age'.

MIKE NICKS
Kettering, Northants

February 1973

Photographs by Nick Nicholls, Malcolm Carling and Brian Holder. Cover picture: Tony Rutter (350 Yamaha) at Silverstone. Inside front cover: Superbike action at Mallory Park. Paul Smart leads Ray Pickrell and Percy Tait, all riding Triumph-3s. Inside back cover: Siegfried Schauzu (BMW), winner of seven TTs, in action on the Mountain circuit. Cover design by Martin Treadway.

The opinions expressed by individual contributors are not necessarily those of the Editor, the publishers, or Castrol Ltd.

CHAPTER 1

Short circuit secrets

by Barry Sheene, leading British and Grand Prix works rider

I'VE RACED in the world championships and I have brief experience of the dollar-heavy American scene. But in my opinion, the most competitive school of road racing in the world is on British short circuits. The riders are among the best you will find anywhere, and they use modern machinery expertly matched to the track requirements. And there are very few easy wins achieved in short circuit competition. Close finishes are commonplace, and you have to ride hard all the way if you're going to be successful.

Like every British rider, I began my career on the short circuits, and I've achieved many of my best results on them. So I'd like to write about the techniques and tactics involved in this form of racing, with special reference to the 250 and 350 cc Yamaha twins which form the backbone of British racing today. The obvious place to begin is on the starting grid.

Starting is one of the most important knacks to learn in British racing, because the races are usually short and hectic. I think I can truthfully say that I'm among the fastest starters, but it's amazing how many quite good riders have trouble in getting away cleanly. And if you have a dozen slower men in front of you, all zooming about on the wrong lines, it can be very difficult to get by.

Oddly enough, almost any rider can start his bike in the paddock at the first attempt. But you'll often see that same rider, using the same technique, completely mess it up when he gets on the grid. They just haven't got the hang of starting consistently well under racing conditions.

This is my technique for the traditional dead-engine start with my Yamahas. In the first place, I make sure that the carburation is running fairly rich at low engine speeds. This ensures that the engine will pick up revs once it fires. I hear a lot of riders say that Yamahas are bad to start, but that's just not true. Most of these people make the mistake of running their motors too lean at the bottom of the rev range. Also, they're afraid to use the flooding lever on the handlebar, in case they gas the engine up completely. If the bike is set up properly, this shouldn't happen.

Admittedly, the transistorised ignition now fitted as standard equipment on Yamahas makes starting a lot easier. These systems give such a strong spark that they will even clear a badly flooded engine, provided you keep pushing the bike. It's the older machines relying on magneto ignition which can be troublesome.

I've seen some riders using a conventional bump start technique to make a Yamaha fire up, but that is a ludicrous waste of time. I take just one step. Then, when my arms are stretched out to the handlebars, I just lean my right side and upper arm on the tank, and that pressure is sufficient to make the rear wheel turn the engine over. The run-and-bump method just is not necessary.

I always try to get my clutch lever out before anyone else's so that I can hear my engine working while there is still silence. Then, as soon as the motor fires, I jump straight into the saddle. This is important because it gives you full control over the bike if you have to do any swerving to avoid slower starters in front.

Dead engine starts are steadily being replaced by clutch starts, but there are some points which apply equally to both methods. You may have noticed, for instance, that I tend to do wheelies accelerating away from the grid on the 250 and 350 cc Yamahas. This is because I whack the throttle right back on to the stop as soon as the engine fires, and control the revs with the clutch lever. Some riders get the clutch home almost immediately, and use the throttle to determine the engine revs, which wastes time because you cannot keep the revs on the power peak.

I just wind the engine up to 11,000 rpm, and ease the clutch out to stop them rising any higher. The wheel starts to come up when I finally let the clutch lever go completely. You can occasionally get caught out, however. Once at Oulton Park I got the front wheel of the 350 up so high that I couldn't see over the nose of the bike. It reared up again when I changed into second, and I had to roll it off to get round the right-hander at the end of the starting straight.

Making full use of one of his consistently good starts, Barry Sheene leads British 350 cc champion Mick Grant (16), world 250 cc champion Jarno Saarinen (17), and former world 125 and 250 cc champion Phil Read at Mallory Park. All are riding Yamahas.

If you can relax on the grid or as you assemble for a clutch start, your grinning and laughing can upset other riders who are tensed up. They'll think, 'How the hell can he joke like that when I'm feeling as bad as this?' This type of rider is also prone to panic as soon as the first engine fires during a dead engine start. He'll think, 'Oh Christ, everyone's going and my motor's not even firing yet!' Then he'll really mess it up.

I must say that I'm not in favour of clutch starts for short circuit racing, even though they seem to be the fashion. They put everyone too close together going into the first corner. If one rider falls in the middle of a bunch of a dozen machines, it can be curtains for everyone.

I must admit I'm biased on this point, though, because I think I'm fairly good at making push starts. I would say that I'm first off the grid nine times out of ten, and I reckon I've made a bad start if I don't get into the first corner among the leading six.

As I see it, the superbikes, which can be heavy to push, are the only machines that really need clutch starts.

But if you make a mess of either a clutch or a push start, the one fatal mistake in short circuit racing is to hang back in the hopes that the slower pack in front of you will sort itself out. It never does, and in the end you find that time is running out and you haven't a hope of getting through to the front. In a situation like this, your only choice is to go as hard as you can for the first couple of laps to try and break through to the leaders.

Once you've made your start, whether it's a good or a bad one, you then have corners to go round and slow down for. Theoretically, I suppose you should do all your braking on a

Another rapid start! This one has developed into a violent wheelie, but at least Barry has time to recover before the pack catches up.

motorcycle while the machine is upright, but in racing it doesn't work out that way. There is always the occasion when you go into a corner faster than you intended, and then you have no alternative but to brake when cranked over. Provided you don't panic and grab a big handful of front anchor you can usually get away with it. Then there are sections of circuits which force you to brake when leaning over even if you're on the right line and doing everything properly. Clearways, on the short circuit at Brands, is a good example of this.

After Cal Rayborn's sensational rides in the 1972 Anglo-American match race series, when he won three of the six races on his four-speed, iron-barrelled Harley-Davidson, there was a lot of talk going round that English riders didn't know how to use their brakes in comparison with the top Americans. There is no doubt that people were impressed at the sight of Calvin whistling up to corners with the wheels of the big Harley on the point of locking, and I suppose there is some truth in the condemnation of British riders.

I can't really explain why the Americans should be such demon brakers, except to point out that their circuits have a lot of straights leading to slow, bottom gear turns. Maybe in this way they get used to using their brakes really hard—I don't know. Certainly I've ridden against Yvon Du Hamel, one of the wildest riders on the American scene, and I know he goes into corners with everything locked up, yet still manages to get round.

But on British short circuits this type of riding does not necessarily pay off. The Esses at Mallory Park are a classic example. Many people would say I'm useless on braking for the right-hander there. But I always slow early for that corner so that I can set the bike up nicely for the following left-hander and get good drive up to the hairpin. So even if someone does outbrake me going into the Esses, I always reckon to get them at the hairpin.

I wouldn't call myself a super braker but, on the other hand, if it's a last lap effort I'll have a go with anyone going into a corner. I like my brakes set up so that my rear one is virtually pathetic. By doing this I can tramp on it fairly hard when I shoot into a corner too fast, yet I know it won't lock.

I also like to set the front brake lever up so that there is plenty of movement before it begins to bite. This is probably one reason why, for the moment at least, I prefer drum brakes to discs. With a hydraulically operated disc brake, it's very difficult to get the lever arranged so that you can pull it a long way before the brake actually starts working. I prefer a longish movement because it gives me more 'feel' in the operation of the brake.

But I admit that I haven't really had a lot of experience with disc brakes. One occasion when I was impressed with a disc set-up was when I rode a Gus Kuhn Commando in the Barcelona 24-hour race around Montjuich Park. That circuit is really hard on brakes, but the NorVil front disc on the Kuhn bike showed no signs of fading even though we kept going for 14 or 15 hours before we retired.

Engine seizures, a dreaded happening with racing two-strokes, are not nearly as common as they used to be. These days manufacturers know a lot more about tolerances and the importance of the shape of the piston in a two-stroke.

Oddly enough, I fell off in my first-ever motorcycle race when my motor nipped up. It was on a 125 cc Bultaco at Brands in 1968. The needle roller bearing on the small end broke up, and the engine just stopped while I was cranked over at Clearways. I cut my lip, took the skin off the palms of my hands, and twisted my foot. But I rode in three more races that afternoon, and after a couple of laps back on the bike I never thought about the possibility of it seizing again.

Since then riding two-strokes has never bothered me, even though I still ride with the fingers of my left hand permanently over the clutch lever, just in case. A common place for an engine to seize is under heavy braking for a corner. In this situation a lot of riders bang down through the gearbox without giving the throttle a blip. What they're really trying to do is find some engine braking, which you can't get on a two-stroke anyway. So their motor is being buzzed really hard at a time when the throttle is shut and there is no petroil going in to lubricate things. Anyone who rides like that must expect an occasional seizure, especially if he has his engine set up to run weak.

To prevent the possibility of the Yams seizing under heavy braking, I usually give the flooding lever a quick flick to give the motor an injection of rich mixture.

I've had two-strokes seize up in some terrible places, and some of the worst times have not been on the short circuits, but in GP racing. I think the most dreadful moment of all was on the 250 cc works Derbi in the 1971 West German GP at Hockenheim. There's a fast right-hander after the starting straight which you take at about 110 mph in fifth. On one lap during practice I'd just got my chin down on to the tank when both cylinders locked up at the same time. That makes you think a bit quick, I can tell you! In the race I made a bad start, but I managed to catch up with Phil Read and Rod Gould, who were

Beside his Team Castrol van, Barry Sheene examines a sparking plug with Yamaha mechanic Nobby Clarke. Clarke is one of the most experienced mechanics in motorcycle racing, and worked with Hondas during their successful ventures in GP racing.

leading on their Yamahas. However, when I was about ten yards behind Rod exactly the same thing happened again, and in exactly the same place, while I was scratching for all I was worth! Both times I just managed to get to the clutch lever before the rear wheel got too far out of line.

In 1972, the crash that messed up most of my season was caused by a seizure. It was in practice for the Italian GP at Imola, and was another of those no-warning jobs, when the piston ring peg came out and jammed in the Yamaha's inlet port. Most two-stroke riders suffer four or five seizures a year, and it's just something you learn to live with. Ray Pickrell, who doesn't like two-strokes, calls them 'hiccup machines'.

For the average short circuit meeting I usually have to ride at about eight-tenths of my maximum possible effort. But I'm always willing to go to ten-tenths when it's necessary. When I first started I could only ride at ten-tenths for a lap or two. But when you have more experience and confidence you can do it almost all the time.

Sometimes you can ride at ten-tenths for a whole race and not have a hairy moment. It was like this for me in 1971 when I had a really good season and everything was going fine. Jarno Saarinen was also able to ride on the edge all the time towards the end of 1972 when he won the 250 cc world championship and came close to beating Agostini and the MV in the 350 class. When you're winning and you're feeling good, you can do it without getting into trouble.

Usually, I try to lay the bike into corners nice and smoothly. Sometimes when you're really having to scratch you just throw it in and get round the corner any way you can. You know before you get halfway round a corner whether or not you're going to run out of road.

On certain corners you can even get the bike into a genuine drift, and at such times you'll feel it move across the road about a foot. A typical example of this occurs on Paddock at Brands. You feel the bike start to drift when you get about halfway round on the downhill bit.

A few years ago there was quite a controversy in short circuit racing about certain riders allegedly 'cutting' people up. I don't know whether that was true or not, but there's hardly anyone who will do it to you these days. I personally, for instance, will hardly ever dive up the inside of someone going into the Mallory Esses. I just don't think it's fair to do that if a bloke's braking as hard as he can and he's got the bike committed to a line. It could throw him too far out to the left for him to get round the following left-hander safely.

The best way to avoid accidents is obviously to keep as far away as you can from other riders—but of course this isn't always possible. I certainly don't like trying to ride round the outside of another rider, because if he comes off he takes you with him. The most dangerous places to go round the outside of people are on first, second and third gear corners, when a rider can easily lose the back wheel by whacking on too much power. Druids Bend at Brands, and the hairpin at Mallory, are typical danger points. At the Mallory hairpin I keep close to the wall on the inside coming out, and get the bike upright as soon as possible. Then I can power it out and there's no danger of the back wheel stepping sideways.

The closest I've ever ridden to another machine was on the final lap of the 125 cc East German GP at the Sachsenring in 1971. I had a fantastic race on my Suzuki with Angel Nieto, who was on the works Derbi. I tried to get round the outside of him on a flat-out right-hander, and there wasn't very much room. We were doing about 90 to 100 mph and our fairings touched. I think we changed places seven times on the last four corners, and on the final bend the crowd thought I had dropped out somewhere because Angel and I were so close together that they couldn't see me. In the end he just won.

If the worst happens and someone falls off when you're close behind, the last thing you do is to panic and grab a big handful of brake. You must ease the throttle and slow down as quickly as you can without locking the wheels.

Getting down to it: Barry Sheene on the 125 cc Suzuki twin on which he finished second in the 1971 world championship . . .

. . . and on the factory 352 cc Yamaha he raced in 1972.

Rain, of course, alters everything. You have to get your choice of line right first time, because it's no good trying to crank it over a bit more when you suddenly realise you're running out of road. If you are going too quickly, it can often be better to deliberately run off the track—where there's room—rather than try to brake and squeeze round. And don't be afraid to stick your feet out if you're in trouble in the wet—it's better to have a red face than a red backside!

You may wonder why I have tended to stay with the smaller machines rather than jump straight on to the 750 cc so-called 'superbikes' as soon as they began to make the headlines in England. But what was the point, when I have always had a 350 or a 500 that's as fast as the big ones? I admit that the BSA and Triumph three-cylinder machines have scored a long run of fantastic successes in Britain, but then the cream of the riders have been racing them—Ray Pickrell, John Cooper, Percy Tait, and Paul Smart, before he left to join Kawasaki in America.

Jarno Saarinen was the guy who really made the superbikes look silly, when he thrashed them on his 350 cc water-cooled Yamaha at Silverstone in 1972. And throughout 1971 I was able to get in among the 'threes' on my 350 Yamaha and on the 500 cc works Suzuki.

The only place where a 350 Yam is really hurting in comparison with the 750s is on acceleration out of really tight bends. The hairpin at Mallory, once again, is a perfect example. I can lose up to 100 yards there on every lap to the BSA and Triumph 750s. They can drive out of the corner without slipping the clutch. But on the Yamaha you have to get it upright before you can feed in the clutch and turn it on.

The four-strokes may have had an advantage in engine braking in the days of single leading shoe brakes, but modern racing brakes are so effective that they have cancelled out this difference.

Yamahas are the mainstay of British short circuit racing these days, just as the Manx Nortons and Matchless G50s once were. And although they look fairly conventional piston-port two-stroke twins, they really are incredible machines, because once you've put one together and fuelled it up you can go straight out and win, whether you're riding at Darley Moor or at the Hutch.

But this is where people begin to make mistakes. The number of riders who will insist on trying to overtune their Yamahas amazes me. There is no excuse for it really, because when you buy a new 250 or 350 cc racing Yamaha you also get a spares kit and a maintenance manual. If you follow that you cannot go wrong. But it's when the 'file freaks' get at engines that the problems start. They will open up an exhaust port so wide you could put your fist in, and then wonder why the piston rings snag the ports and break.

These people would cry if they realised just how little work went into my TD2 and TR2 Yamahas in 1971, for example. In about 15 meetings the TR2 must have won a dozen races and smashed a couple of lap records. Yet when I sold it towards the end of the season it was still running on the original barrels and pistons. Later I got stuck for a machine and had to borrow it back from the new owner, and on it I won the King of Brands title.

That same year, my 250 cc TD2 was in a bad state when I got back from the Finnish GP for the big autumn internationals in Britain, but I only had time to replace a faulty gear cluster and make sure that the motor was set up correctly. Even though it was still running on the same pistons, barrels and crankshaft that I had been using in the GPs, it then won four international 250 cc races at the Hutch, Silverstone, the Race of the Year, and the Race of the South.

Finally, some words on that vital factor, a rider's mental outlook. Obviously, some races attract better entries than others. But whatever the event, I try to line up at the start with an open mind as to the outcome. I think it's very important never to decide beforehand that you can't win. In fact, I never allow myself to settle for second or third place before the race has started. When the bikes are lining up, I always try to think, 'I have a reasonable chance of success'. I know this may sound like an obvious attitude for a professional rider to take, but it's surprising how many top men allow themselves to get beaten before the race has started.

Similarly, there are other riders who will go well for a few laps and then run out of steam. You can afford to sit behind these people early in a race, knowing that sooner or later they will slow. I could reel off a list of names of such riders—but I won't, since I don't like to make unnecessary enemies!

I never find myself feeling aggressive towards other riders on the track. Obviously, if someone comes past me I'll hang on and try to repass. But I never get evil about it. I think a lot of riders do tend to become aggressive when they're being beaten, but in my opinion it's a mistake to get like that. You get hairy and carried away, and you start taking unnecessary risks. There's a world of difference between riding hard and riding angrily.

Anyway, I think you really have to enjoy racing for its own sake before you can be successful at it, and I certainly find plenty of pleasurable things in racing. To me, my motorcycle racing career means three things—success, popularity, and then money. In that order.

Champion and challenger: Jarno Saarinen and Barry Sheene on the grid at Mallory Park.

CHAPTER 2

Running a works team

by Frank Perris, Team Manager, John Player Nortons

FOR THE LAST FEW YEARS of my racing career, the thought of running a works team had been high on my list of interesting jobs that I wanted to tackle. So when the chance came to do just this for the magical name of Norton, with the backing of John Player's sponsorship, I felt a very happy and contented man.

I've always been concerned about the image of motorcycle racing, and even in my novice days I realised that there was very much more to being a successful motorcycle racer than just riding a machine quickly. And when Formula 1 car racing began to benefit from the advent of large-scale sponsorship, I decided that that was the sort of promotion and publicity which motorcycling needed so much. When the Japanese bowed out of the sport during the latter half of the 'sixties, road racing seemed to lose much of its prestige. The Japanese had acted as their own travelling promotional organisations. They left an aura wherever they went, and although I was proud to be a member of one of those teams, it grieved me to think that the Japanese had to show us how to do it.

Now, after a few years of doldrums, a new partnership has been born into the sport which I am firmly convinced will lead the way towards motorcycle racing being accepted by the general public as a major spectacle. It's really a three-way partnership, the members being Norton, John Player and the Formula 750 racing class.

It's all excitingly new—Norton back with a works team after 15 years out of the sport, the vast promotional resources of John Player, and Formula 750, a class where the man in the street can see engines similar to the motor in his own road bike built into GP chassis and competing against factory teams from Europe, Japan and America.

Formula 750 was born in the USA and brought to Europe by promoter Chris Lowe, of Motor Circuit Developments, Neville Goss, Britain's go-ahead member of the FIM's sporting committee, and the BSA-Triumph organisation. Unfortunately, none of the foreign factories at first chose to compete against BSA in this country, so it was a considerable boost to the sport when the John Player Norton team came along at the beginning of 1972. Although we did not have a wholly successful first season, I'm sure that the racing would have been a lot less exciting if we hadn't been there.

But first, let me return to the beginning of what is still very recent history. Once the John Player-Norton link had been forged, we held a company meeting in the first week of December 1971 to decide what type of machine we would field. Obviously, the 750 cc ohv

14   CASTROL MOTORCYCLE RACING MANUAL

Two theories on streamlining: above, by John Player Norton (rider Peter Williams); below, by Ducati (rider Paul Smart).

twin-cylinder Commando engine, on which Norton Villiers base their range of road machines, would form the power unit. But what we had to determine was whether the engine should be fitted into a GP-type chassis, which Formula 750 rules allow, or whether we should use stripped-down versions of the Commando production racer.

Both Peter Williams and I opted to build GP frames, because we knew they would be more competitive. But there was some opposition to this idea, for it was felt that there was insufficient time to produce the frames before the season began. Our proposal was eventually agreed on, however. This left us with only nine working weeks before the first event of the season, the Daytona 200 in March 1972. I got together with Peter, who is the team's development engineer as well as a rider, and we drew up a week-by-week schedule which had to be adhered to. We knew that the programme was so tight that, if we once slipped behind, we would never be able to recover the lost time.

One very fortunate factor acted as our saviour. Peter, of course, had been working at Norton Villiers and racing the Commandos for some time before the John Player team was formed. During this period he had drawn up a design for a new racing frame intended purely for his own use. This meant that once the decision was made for Nortons to field a full works team, we had a ready-made frame design to draw on.

Finally, with great help from the main Norton Villiers factory at Wolverhampton, we were able to fly the bikes out from our racing headquarters at Andover to Florida. There, at Daytona, Phil Read raced the bike into fourth place in its very first outing.

That success in a very tough, 200-mile marathon certainly made us feel good, but at the same time it didn't fool us. We had seen, for example, that most other factory machines had retired—Phil was, in fact, the first works rider home behind three privately entered 350 cc Yamahas. As it turned out, we went on to suffer plenty of troubles later in the season, but I can't remember a single factory team which hasn't had its share of problems in its first year of racing.

I was really surprised and pleased at the number of people who came up during that first season and said how glad they were to see Nortons back in racing and that they were literally willing us to score our first major win. We even had rival riders like John Cooper and Ray Pickrell behind us! They would tell us how genuinely happy they would be to see us win a big event. I must say that when it finally happened, with Peter Williams' fine defeat of Paul Smart and the works Ducati in the *Evening News* race at the Hutchinson 100, John Cooper came up afterwards and told me: 'There you are, mate, I knew you'd do it some time this year. No one is more pleased than me'. I really appreciated that sentiment from one of our main competitors. Later in the year, Mick Grant gave us another big win in the Scarborough round of the *Motor Cycle News* Superbike series, and Phil Read won the Race of the South at Brands.

There was also a certain disadvantage in having a sponsor such as John Player, in that so many people immediately expected so much from us. The number of those who wished us well was equalled by the critics who would inform us: 'I just can't understand why you're not getting anywhere, with all that backing you have'. But, in racing, money doesn't automatically buy success, even if you have an unlimited budget—and we have to work to a very tight one.

To those who felt we were slow to achieve success, I would say this: think back to when the Japanese teams first entered racing. They all suffered lean years at the beginning. But they were never criticised at that time, because few people in Europe really knew of the multi-million pound industrial empires that were behind those early attempts. If the public over here had realised that, no doubt they might have offered meagre judgement on the first Japanese efforts in road racing.

Through all this, the John Player people remained helpful and sympathetic. When you enjoy the backing of a major sponsor, press receptions and similar functions become a part of life, but we were always asked to attend these at times when work at Andover was not at its most hectic. The only exception was when the BBC made a 25-minute television film of the team's involvement in the 1972 Anglo-American match races. For two days the television people virtually took over our workshops at a time when we were really pressed to prepare the bikes for the races. But the trouble was well worth it, because of the value of that film in promoting motorcycle sport. It was transmitted late one afternoon during the children's programmes on BBC-1, and it must have made thousands of mums realise that the people who work in motorcycle racing are not greasy haired hooligans.

Since our team is the first in motorcycling to win the assistance of a big sponsor— although this type of liaison is commonplace in car racing these days—I'd like to describe how the arrangement works. I am not, for instance, told who I must choose as team riders, or what technical changes must be made to the machines before the next race—far from it. At the beginning of the year, a contract is negotiated between the sponsor and Dennis Poore, the chairman of Norton Villiers. For that first year, the main agreement was that we would undertake to contest the 750 cc Superbike championship and other international events in this country. We also raced at the Imola 200-miler in Italy and in America's Daytona 200 and Ontario classics, but this was purely our own decision, since John Player did not market in those countries. Our sponsors also asked that we paint the bikes and transporters in their colours, that we wear the team livery when at race meetings and associated functions, and that we generally conduct our operations in a businesslike manner. That,

Dunlop tyre designer Tony Mills (left) and competitions manager David Shaw (second left) discuss problems with Frank Perris, rider Tony Rutter, and mechanic Peter Pykett (right).

really, is as far as the contract extends. The choice of riders, the design of the machines, the configuration of our engines—all these major decisions are left to Norton personnel.

As it happened, we earned plenty of publicity for our sponsors, even though we did not enjoy a fantastic season from the point of view of race wins. This, I think, is an indication of the indifferent manner in which teams and individual riders have been promoting themselves in recent years. You'll sometimes see a talented rider sitting in the back of a battered van eating beans out of a can and moaning: 'Why can't they pay me more start money?'. How do they expect to get really good money when they cannot even present themselves to race organisers and spectators in an attractive manner?

The value and the need for promotion was really brought home to me during the six years from 1961 to 1966 when I raced as a Suzuki works rider. As I've already suggested, the big Japanese teams of those days were literally travelling sales promotion equipes. The Suzuki mechanics would never be seen in anything other than clean overalls, and the riders would all wear team anoraks. We never got round to wearing team leathers, because at that time no one had thought of using any other colour than black. But the factory's demands for a good image even extended into the personal behaviour of riders and mechanics. You dare not get involved in paddock punch-ups or incidents of that kind if you wanted to stay in the team.

I learnt so much from those exciting years that today I find it no hardship—the very opposite, in fact—to apply those lessons to the workings of the John Player Norton team.

John Player Nortons on the front row at Brands. From left, Mick Grant (JPN), Peter Williams (JPN), Bruno Spaggiari (750 Ducati), Ray Pickrell (750 Triumph), Phil Read (JPN), Paul Smart (750 Ducati) and Dave Croxford (750 Seeley-BSA).

Mick Grant celebrates with supergirls after his Norton win at the Scarborough Superbike round in 1972.

I'm trying to get our operation running very much on the lines of the former Japanese GP teams. I want to pare our organisation down so that it's highly efficient, with every member of the team knowing his exact functions in the set-up. The Japanese were very adept at this sort of planning, and would achieve considerable results and output with a relatively small number of people. Under this system, everything is schemed to a timetable, so that you always know what targets you have to meet.

Readers who were following GP racing in the mid-'sixties may recall that in 1964 and 1965 Suzuki took 20 mechanics to the Isle of Man. That may sound wasteful, but remember that those men had to look after no less than 22 machines split between the 50, 125 and 250 cc classes, and shared among seven factory riders—three Japanese and four Europeans. So no one found he had time on his hands.

Our team at Thruxton is made up of eight mechanics—two men who build the race engines, four who build the bikes, a machinist, and a frame builder—development engineer Peter Williams, a draughtsman, a secretary, a work chaser—that's a man who makes sure that when outside materials are ordered, they arrive on time—and myself.

We receive standard Commando engines from Wolverhampton, and we strip them down and reassemble them to our own specifications. In our first year we relied almost entirely on standard components, and when we went to Daytona our engine was giving just 69 bhp —only 4 bhp more than the Combat engine in a road-going Commando. Naturally, during the season, we experimented with items such as camshafts, carburettors, induction lengths, port shapes, valve sizes and exhaust systems, and by the end of the year we had engines that were giving 76 to 77 bhp at 7,500 rpm. But it was surprising how many production components we used. This policy ensured that the ordinary Commando rider on the road could still relate his machine to our John Player Nortons out on the circuits.

John Player Nortons at work on Scarborough's narrow and bumpy 'little TT' circuit. Above, Mick Grant (7) and Peter Williams swing into Mere hairpin. Below, the Nortons accelerate away into the shadows.

We're fairly self-sufficient and versatile down at Thruxton, even to the extent of making our own fuel and oil tanks and seats. The fuel tanks are almost works of art, for they are hand-beaten from alloy into a quite complex shape. Apart from the wheels, forks, rear suspension units and the fairing, almost everything on the bike is manufactured either at Thruxton or at Wolverhampton.

Screen and Plastic make the glass fibre fairings, and Barry Johnson of Amal and Geoff Johnson of Lucas have given tremendous help with carburettors and electronic ignition, respectively. To gain more power, we switched from Amal GP carburettors to Concentrics, and the Concentrics we now use are specially made for us by Amal. They have no identification markings on the bodies, so that no one else knows what size they are.

We also build our own frames at Thruxton, and it says a lot for Peter's ability that throughout the year we left the basic geometry of the bikes exactly as it had been when his design first came off the drawing board. It was not perfect, and Peter is the first to admit this. It made the bikes a little heavy on the front end, and correspondingly light at the rear. The result was that our riders could not turn on the power quite as quickly as their rivals on the BSA-Triumph machines. If they did, the back end would try to step out.

Peter's design retained the large-diameter backbone section of the road-going Commando models, but the entire frame was scaled down. It kept the Commando's rubber-mounted engine, and also the road bike's method of locating the swinging arm in the engine plates behind the gearbox. The whole concept of the John Player Nortons is that they should be very low and compact, presenting a small frontal area. But we had to sacrifice an inch in height by going from 18-inch to 19-inch wheels. This was to gain more ground clearance, for we found that the bikes were dragging when heeled over in corners. But the only occasion when this caused a rider to fall was, we believe, during tests with Tony Rutter at Brands Hatch before the season began. For 1973, of course, we changed to a monocoque frame design, which gave us an even lower machine.

We used NorVil front disc brakes, and not the Norton Lockheed units fitted to the roadster Commandos. This is because the NorVil discs are an inch greater in diameter, at 11 in, although the Norton Lockheed brakes are quite capable of dealing with the speeds of ordinary road bikes. We used both twin and single discs on the front wheel, the choice being entirely up to the riders. Phil Read went for twin discs every time, because he likes his brakes to respond to the least effort on the lever. But Peter stayed with a single disc, because he prefers to use more lever pressure.

Oil coolers were not designed into the original bikes, but we fitted them almost as soon as we arrived at our first meeting at Daytona. Without them, the engines were running far too hot. Originally, we mounted the cooler in the tail of the machine. Later in the season we located it in the nose of the fairing, and cut a slot in the fairing to act as an air inlet to the radiator. This change of positioning alone reduced the oil temperature by something like 30 deg C.

As another aid to more power, we changed from a siamesed exhaust system to two separate pipes. Modifications like this saw us gradually adding weight, and we eventually finished up with bikes weighing about 350 lbs. But really we had to make very few major changes to the machines during the season.

It was no secret that continual gearbox failures formed our greatest problems—the engines themselves proved very reliable. The main trouble with the transmission was that it did not enjoy the benefits of a shock absorber, either on the crankshaft or in the rear hub. The gearbox could not withstand the resultant stresses, and it took us some time to discover all this. But after experiments with Norton-made gearboxes and with the excellent clusters made by the specialist gearbox manufacturer Rod Quaife, we eventually built shock absorbers into the transmission, and this solved the problems.

We were also handicapped in that first year by being down on power compared with

John Cooper, who gave the John Player Norton team considerable encouragement in their first year, shares a joke with team manager Frank Perris. Cooper is now a team rider.

most other manufacturers who were contesting Formula 750 racing. But I remain firmly convinced that there is a great future in Formula 750 for twin-cylinder machines, even though there are so many exotic multi-cylinder designs around these days, such as the three-cylinder water-cooled Suzuki. Our feelings on the advantages of a twin-cylinder machine were amply supported in the 1972 Anglo-American match races, when Cal Rayborn showed everyone the way round on his V-twin Harley-Davidson, which even had cast iron cylinder barrels.

A twin cannot match the out-and-out power developed by machines like the three-cylinder Suzukis and Kawasakis. But there is much more than brute force at stake when you are trying to build a fast motorcycle. One of the main formulae for speed is to ensure that your machine has to push a low frontal area through the air. At speeds of about 140 or 150 mph, a motorcycle needs one extra bhp for every additional mile an hour of speed—so you can see how vital is this argument for a low frontal area. Reducing the frontal area can be just as fruitful in terms of speed gained as finding more power from the engine. We have proved this at Daytona and at the TT. At Daytona, when none of our machines was giving more than 69 bhp at the crankshaft, Phil Read was timed through the speed trap at 155.17 mph. This was well down on the Suzukis, one of which was timed at 171.75 mph. But it equalled the fastest trap speed recorded in 1971, by Ginger Molloy's 500 cc Kawasaki, and it was 4.17 mph better than the highest speed ever recorded on the combined banking and road course at Daytona up to then by a BSA-Triumph 'three', which stood to Mike Hailwood in 1971. In the TT in 1972 Peter Williams took one of our bikes through the Highlander speed trap at 148.8 mph; BSA-Triumph's best was Ray Pickrell's 146.9.

The theory of designing a low frontal area is by no means new, and Moto Guzzi knew the secret of it years ago. They won the 350 cc world championship back in 1956 with a low and light single-cylinder machine which had its engine mounted horizontally to save height. Even when they were racing the fantastic V8 500 in 1957, Guzzi still believed sufficiently in the 'low and light' formula to field a single-cylinder 500 for slower circuits.

In Formula 750 I am convinced that the designer who can get 85 bhp to the rear wheel from a twin-cylinder machine with a low frontal area will have a winner. It might be at a disadvantage trying to beat the 117 bhp of the three-cylinder Suzukis on a very fast circuit, but even then it could be a better bet if it was made light enough and low enough. In Europe, circuits like Hockenheim and Spa will favour bikes with the greatest power, but there again my theoretical 85 horsepower twin could still be as quick.

It's quite possible to prove these claims from data the Norton team has obtained during experiments in the Motor Industry Research Association's wind tunnel. In fact, Peter Williams has compiled a very useful graph on the subject. From it we can work out how much horsepower we need, given the frontal area of a machine, to reach, say, 175 mph—a speed we shall certainly have to achieve some time in 1973 if we are going to be competitive.

We are fortunate at Nortons in that both Peter and I share the same beliefs in this light weight, low profile theory, and at the same time we work for a factory that produces twin-cylinder motorcycles. Even if there were no requirement to use a production engine as a basis in modern 750 cc racing, and manufacturers could use as many cylinders as they desired, I would still choose a twin-cylinder design. My feelings on the subject are generated by a lifetime of experience gained in motorcycle racing. I have very vivid memories, for example, of the 250 cc 'square fours' that Suzuki produced in the mid-'sixties. In their ultimate form, they gave 66 bhp at the gearbox, and had a top speed of about 145 mph. In those days, that was really something for a 250. But it was very apparent from riding those machines that their design was based solely on gaining horsepower and top speed. There was very little concern for anything that happened on the bits between the straights.

Spectators are always drawn by the smart, professional appearance of the Norton machinery and personnel.

Peter Williams enjoys a different kind of Norton, in company with television personality Jon Pertwee in a damp Brighton run. Peter is riding a 1912 490 cc Norton, his partner a 1914 348 cc Royal Enfield.

Consequently, the handling was so bad that Jack Ahearn, one of the team riders, christened the bikes 'Whispering Death'. He got the nickname from the fact that you could hardly hear the bikes when they were coming towards you. The square fours nearly killed old Jack, and a lot of people who rode them had bad accidents. I smashed my leg on one at Daytona, Ernst Degner crashed one and burnt himself horribly on the face and chest, and they scared Hughie Anderson so much that he refused to ride them.

They were some of the quickest bikes around in any class, but they were spoilt by too much concentration on one aspect of the machine—power. They were introduced in 1963, but the best result they ever achieved was the third place I scored in the 1965 TT. They were eventually scrapped at the end of that year.

My preference for the lighter, less complex type of machine was reinforced before I joined Suzuki, when I rode the works AJS 7R 350 and the Matchless G45 500 in the mid-'fifties. At that time I also worked with Peter Williams' father Jack, the famous development engineer with Associated Motor Cycles.

The selection of riders is one of the team manager's major functions, and it's not such a straightforward job as it might seem, for you must look for more qualities in a man than the basic ability to get round a circuit quickly. He must be consistent. I could name plenty of riders who are very fast around their one favourite circuit, but a factory team needs men who can lap quickly on any type of track. He must be intelligent. In a works team, there may be occasions when one of your riders is leading a particular championship. In such a case, his team-mates must have the foresight to realise that they must guard his chances of winning the title, even at the expense of their own successes. I also like to know how a rider reacts after he's flung the machine down the road. If he wants to walk away and retire, he probably hasn't got the hardened professional attitude which he needs to survive the pressures of riding in a works team.

If the team is backed by a major sponsor, a rider must also acquire a degree of self-assurance to carry him through the social occasions he will be asked to attend. I also watch for a rider's influence on the mechanics. Some riders have that special quality in their personalities that makes it a pleasure to prepare bikes for them. This was really brought home to me at the 1972 TT, when we were having a lot of problems, especially with the gearboxes, and the mechanics were working 16 or 17 hours a day. John Cooper was riding for us in that event, and whenever he came into the garage he would laugh with us and joke, and subtly boost everyone's ego. John later joined the team, of course, while Phil Read and Mick Grant left when we decided to cut back to two riders.

Of all the events in a season's racing, I still feel that the TT is the most demanding on a works team. If you send a bike out for two practice laps of the 37¾-mile Mountain circuit, it completes the equivalent of all the training and racing it does in an entire short circuit meeting on the mainland. Then there are other difficulties, such as shipping the team over there. The Isle of Man Steam Packet Co gives absolutely no preference to the people who present the show at the TT, so if you haven't booked your vans on the boats for the June races before Christmas, it's almost impossible to get over there.

But I really like the TT. I'm afraid I'm one of the old school, and if I was still racing I would feel more at home on the TT circuit than on a British short circuit. After 1956 I didn't race much in England, but concentrated on the GPs. So I really got to enjoy racing on natural road circuits. Today, as a team manager, I still feel that the TT is an important race to win, because an awful lot of people continue to use it as the ultimate yardstick of a racing motorcycle.

I believe that Formula 750 racing is going to become even more competitive than GP racing used to be. In the 250 cc class of the GPs, for instance, it used to be pretty obvious that the reason that firms like Benelli, CZ and MZ could not match the Japanese was certainly that they didn't have people capable of designing good bikes. It was a question of pure finance, or lack of it. But the Formula 750 ruling which says that you must produce 200 units of an engine before you can race it puts an end to the so-called 'freak' power units, and helps the relatively smaller companies to compete with the giants such as Suzuki, Yamaha and Kawasaki.

Even though Formula 750 relies on 'production' engines, I still feel that it offers tremendous engineering and technical challenges. It must be very satisfying, for example, for Suzuki's engineers to sit back and enjoy the thought that they have coaxed up to 117 bhp from their three-cylinder water-cooled 750, when it is basically a road machine engine. In any case, if 750 cc racing was run to an 'anything goes' GP formula, I honestly don't think the bikes would be going that much quicker, because we've now arrived at the stage where frame design is lagging behind engine power outputs. There is no doubt that Formula 750 is going to present a truly fantastic spectacle once it gets its own world championship, and I hope that the Norton works team will be right in there in the front of the struggle.

CHAPTER 3

How much does it cost?

by Chris Carter, circuit commentator and BBC correspondent

A VERY WELL KNOWN ROAD RACER, who had better remain nameless, was once asked what advice he would give to someone about to enter the sport. 'Take up golf,' was his instant reply!

But assuming you are not filled with wild enthusiasm about knocking a little ball across a field with the aid of a metal club, and instead have visions of replacing Giacomo Agostini as 500 cc world champion, there's one thing you should be quite clear about: there are no short cuts to fame in any branch of motorcycle sport. Trials, moto cross, speedway or road racing, whatever the name of your particular game, you will have to start at the bottom rung of that hard and tough ladder of success.

If road racing is the branch of two-wheeled sport that has caught your imagination, then you will have to start in club meetings. There is no other way. And if all the road racing you have seen is at Mallory Park and Brands Hatch national meetings, or at the Isle of Man TT, then let's quickly dispel any suggestions that club racing is full of no-hope novices, riding on machines that were bought by courtesy of the local junk shop. Today club racing in Britain is a highly competitive sport, with many riders combining success at national level with club events.

At Darley Moor, in Derbyshire, for example there are two regular competitors who won rounds of the 1972 British road racing championships, yet they are still beaten from time to time! Machinery, too, can range from the cheapest to the latest £1,000-plus Yamaha. Sometimes it is difficult to tell whether you are in the paddock at a national meeting or a club day. The standard of machine preparation and the variety of models are much the same.

How long you stay racing at club level depends on many things, of course. But you must complete at least six events in order to qualify for a national licence. In England, like many other countries, qualification for national, and later, international licences is based on performances at the lower level. The fee for a national licence is just £1, but your application form has to be countersigned by a club secretary, who confirms that you have started, 'raced satisfactorily' and finished in six club meetings on at least two different circuits.

It will cost you, then, much more than that £1 licence fee, before you make your first appearance in a British road racing championship round, or in any other national permit meeting, for that matter. How much it will cost depends on many things—and not least of all on you, or rather, on your shape! It is not sound practice, though not impossible, for a 6 ft 4 in 16-stone giant to race a 50, for example. And maybe it is not wise, to start with anyway, for an 8-stone, 5 ft tall weakling to be let loose with a 750 cc Triumph-3.

Your financial state will be another determining factor. What machine you can afford to buy and maintain depends on the size of your wage packet. Without wishing to frighten off any potential Mike Hailwoods, because we need you, do not run away with the idea that a start in road racing can be achieved by the supreme sacrifice of giving up one packet of cigarettes a week. If you are not prepared to go without many of the usual pleasures of life, then road racing is not for you. How much sacrifice you make depends on how many meetings you want to ride in each season, and how far your ambitions stretch.

But we are putting the cart before the horse. Let's buy the bike first. Like all commodities, the price of a racing motorcycle fluctuates with supply and demand. The best time to buy is at the end of the season when riders want to sell their old bikes in order to buy new mounts for the following year. If you wait till the start of the season prices may have risen slightly, although there is the exception to this rule when a rider who has been unable to sell his last year's machine is becoming desperate as the opening season nears, and his new model needs paying for. But 'buy in autumn' is still the golden rule, for not only will the price usually be better, but you will have the close season to strip it down, see what makes it tick, and replace the parts that need replacing.

DON'T be fooled by the sort of advertisement that claims a machine is 'ex-Sheene', 'ex-Chatterton', or 'ex-Cooper'. A bike raced long ago by a superstar can still be a very well worn machine.

DON'T buy a machine that will be too fast for you. To start with a bike of which you are the complete master is a much better idea. The time to buy a quicker model is when you feel you are running out of steam down the straights—not when you're still learning to hang on to the bars of your existing model.

DON'T be afraid to ask. Even superstars are human, and generally any road racer, at the right time, will be pleased to give advice and help to someone keen on taking up the

The 496 cc Seeley G50 single-cylinder racer has now gone out of production, but is still a popular machine with many club riders. The 90×78 mm engine features a chain-driven overhead camshaft.

sport. But the right time is not just before the start of a race, or while he is busy trying to repair his machine! You cannot buy experience, that's true. But the pitfalls of road racing are well known to riders who have been competing for even a short time. A few words of wisdom from someone who knows can save you time and money.

It's an impossible task for me to suggest the sort of machine you should buy. Instead let's examine what a season's racing has cost a few club road racers over a range of solo and sidecar mounts. Then you can make up your own mind.

Fifty cc racing is very much a specialist cult. Regrettably, fewer and fewer circuits cater for these machines at national level, but at club meetings, there's still plenty of enthusiasm and opportunities to race. Costs of machines here range from well below three figures to £400 and £500 for ex-works models from manufacturers such as Kreidler, Derbi and Jamathi. The more exotic the machine, the greater your chance of success. But remember, spares can be both expensive and rare. If you want to go 50 cc racing, forget the works bikes, and aim instead for a Honda, Suzuki or Kreidler.

The Honda CR110 introduced in the early 'sixties was a superbly engineered production road racer. The eight-speed double overhead cam engine, although only available at first to selected riders, has put success and reliability within reach of anyone. Costing around £400 new, a good one at the present time can be bought for about £200. Nigel Stone, the Leicester 50 cc racer who was the only Englishman to score world championship points in this class in 1972, started his career among the tiddlers on a second-hand CR110 Honda. In two years of racing, with considerable success, the machine, apart from the usual maintenance of changing the engine oil and piston rings, cost Nigel almost nothing in new parts.

The RS50 Suzuki production racer, another Japanese model of the early 'sixties, is also a reasonably priced competitive machine for this class. Current prices are in line with second-hand Honda CR110s, while the latest road-going Suzuki engine, with a race kit conversion, can cost around £500.

But perhaps best value of all for someone setting out in 50 cc racing is gained by buying a Kreidler motor available in standard trim with a five-speed, close-ratio gearbox, and having it converted by Dutchman Theo Moeurs into a disc valve, water-cooled unit with

Club racers pictured at Croft circuit, in Yorkshire, where several top riders have begun their careers.

six speeds, for around £300. All you need to do, then, is slot the engine into a frame. Altogether that little lot could come to nearly £600! Just because they are small, 50 cc road race machines are not necessarily cheap. But with a little care and consideration they can provide an inexpensive and surprisingly fast form of two-wheeled sport.

Neil Stafford, a teenager from Derbyshire, started his racing career on a road-going 125 cc Yamaha YAS1. New, it cost him around £200. But after just a few miles on the road and four outings in standard trim at nearby Darley Moor club meetings, it was converted to racing specification. He spent £30 on a better front brake, because there is no point in making something go faster if you cannot stop it quickly. To give more power, a local workshop wizard worked on the porting and the compression ratio. You can expect to pay about £10 for that. Racing tyres took £28, expansion chambers another £30. A racing tank, seat and fairing put a further £55 on the bill. So Neil was in business after spending about £150 on the conversion

That first year's racing, including the machine and its modification, set Neil back nearly £700. Where did the other £350 go after the bike had been bought and modified? Entry fees, including club subscriptions, came to £75. Petrol for the machine cost £25. Travel expenses totalled £45. Racing tyres added another £50 to the bill, and new racing leathers, boots, gloves and a Bell helmet when he first started came to another £65. It's safe to allow around £3 a meeting for entry fees, insurance and club subscriptions. Add another £3 for petrol for the bike and your transporter for each meeting, and it's easy to see that an outlay of over £10 a meeting is easily reached. During the first year, the Yamaha was a model of reliability. But during the second, as Neil raced the machine harder and parts wore out, repair bills came along. He spent more than £150 on spares in that second season. For his money, though, Neil was a regular racer. Most weekends he was out at least once, and often twice, with success, too.

If the 'little' bikes don't appeal to you, then try a 250 or 350 cc Yamaha. Costs for either one of these high speed Japanese two-strokes are much the same. John Newbold, another Derbyshire teenager, started racing in 1971 in the 250 cc class. He bought a TD1B Yamaha for £290, and spent a further £90 on converting it to TD1C specification, the extra money going on new expansion chambers, barrels and pistons, and Amal Concentric carburettors.

Replacing piston rings and little ends every three or four meetings at a cost of about £4 a time kept repair bills low. But allowing £60 for entry fees and club subscriptions, John's first season of 18 meetings cost him about £500, including petrol for the bike and transport costs. When he changed the 250 for a £700 350 cc TR2 the following season, John's expenses rose as he raced more often. Two new big ends and a seizure in the first half of the 1972 season took repair bills to more than £300. Including the cost of his machine, Newbold spent almost £1,500 in nearly 40 meetings in his second season. That meant an average of £20 a meeting on repairs, fuel, entry fees and other general expenses. When he realised this John was staggered! Yet he keeps accurate records of his running costs, so riders who don't keep 'accounts' could be in for even bigger shocks.

But racing isn't always that expensive. Tony Johnson retired at the end of the 1972 season after a career that started in 1953 in Australia, and had continued with moderate success ever since. Pressure of work limited his racing to about a dozen meetings in each of the last couple of seasons that he raced. With an elderly, much modified 500 cc Manx Norton Tony made reliability his keynote instead of speed, and kept his season's outlay to about £120, or about £10 a meeting. Over a year, that's only just over £2 a week, not counting the purchase cost of his racer. It shows that even on a shoe-string, racing is possible.

Why does Tony go for reliability instead of performance? The answer is simple. He races for pleasure, and feels it's better to go the full distance in a race for which you have

Nigel Stone has enjoyed success in club racing on his 50 cc Jamathi. Right, Lance Capon goes to the other end of the scale, with his 1,000 cc Vincent.

paid your entry fee, even at a slightly slower pace, than be forced to quit after two laps of high speed circulation.

If the choice is a new chain or a high performance cam, go for the chain—that's Tony's advice to the newcomer. This is where his £120 went. Subscription and entry fees for 12 months, £36; petrol for the machine and travelling costs, £30; tyres, plugs, chains and clutch plates, £34. That left £20 or so for repairs during the season.

That's racing on the cheap, for sure, and it's generally on the older British four-strokes that this sort of economy is possible. But don't spend your money on the 350 cc 7R AJS or on 350 cc Manx Nortons. They are no longer competitive, while in the 500 and 750 cc classes big four-strokes that won't cost a fortune to buy can still be in with a chance of a placing. They can also give trouble-free racing.

Tony also advises against making false economies. Second-hand racing tyres are usually not much use, and by the time you have wasted time and temper mending punctures, you would have been better off investing in a new set of tyres and tubes at the start of the season.

This is the sort of labour-saving hint that is useful to newcomers to racing. For even with the best behaved racing motorcycle routine work and maintenance can take up a lot of time. Anything that helps cut out unnecessary jobs must be good. It has been claimed that for every minute spent racing, you should invest an hour of work on the bike—an exaggeration, maybe, but one that's not far short of the truth.

The bigger solo classes and production machine racing have the same sort of appeal to the would-be racer as the 500 cc British single-cylinder machines. And in production events it is possible, in theory at least, to race the same machine that you ride to work. You can even ride it to meetings, although this is not really a sound plan. A major blow-up, or even a crash, can leave you unhurt, but without transport home.

The ease of tuning, reasonable cost of spares, and the reliability of somewhat older twin-cylinder machines from the major British factories make unlimited cc racing at most club meetings one of the most competitive and enjoyable of all classes. But don't run before you can walk. A big bike, in racing fettle, can be a handful. So, too, can 250 and 350 cc Yamahas. Start with a motorcycle that you are sure you can master. It's easy enough to move on to quicker bikes later. If you are always in awe of your bike, then your racing won't be so enjoyable, and it will take you that much longer to improve.

Perhaps it's not two wheels that turn you on, but three? Well, sidecar racing has plenty to recommend it. The comradeship between the chair racers is well known, and if you have a friend who is keen to act as ballast, then expenses and the work can be shared. But make sure the person you split the expense with really is a good friend, and not someone who is likely to lose interest halfway through the season. It is not a sound plan to have to sell your outfit midway through the year because the person who owns half of it wants to take up tiddly-winks!

It is possible, and it frequently happens, that a solo road race machine can be built and raced successfully by the man who wants to go racing. But with sidecars it's a rather more difficult and dangerous way to go about it. The best plan is to watch racing and note the outfits that appear to handle well. If, and when, one of them comes up for sale, then the purchase of a complete outfit could be a cheaper way of breaking into sidecar racing in the long run. The power unit for a sidecar is purely a matter of choice, but few experienced men would argue that for beginners a Triumph engine is the best bet. Even though spares are becoming a little less plentiful than before and are therefore a shade dearer, the cost of an average Triumph blow-up of the sort that a first season sidecar racer could expect, shouldn't set him back more than about £25-£30.

Mick Gillett, from Ockbrook in Derbyshire, started racing with a 650 Triumph outfit that cost him £130. But though, as with many sidecar men, retirements were a little above par for the first year, stoppages were generally the result of minor problems. Apart from a new set of clutch plates, new chains, and—if you are a hard rider—new tyres midway through the season, spares shouldn't cost very much. As with other branches of road racing, entry fees and club subscriptions are one of the major items of expense during the season. Although a solo rider can allow just £3 a meeting for these items, insurance for the two men on an outfit can lift that figure to perhaps £4 a meeting. When you feel ready to move on to a better outfit, then an outlay of £300 to £400 is probably the price you will have to pay. For super-fast outfits, sums of double that are not unusual.

Remember that a 'bargain' racer, whether for the solo or sidecar classes, can be far from that. A cheap machine could need a small fortune spent on it to put it into raceworthy condition. It's better to buy something a little more expensive that in the long run will save you money. Where do you seek advice on all this? Obviously, at road race meetings. But if an opportunity doesn't exist for you to find your way into the race paddock, join a good motorcycle club, and ask the people there.

To see once, is better than to hear a thousand times, is a very true saying. To race once, is better than to spectate a thousand times. So if you think you have what it takes, the only way is to have a go. But there is a simple short cut that could perhaps save you time and money. Several road racing schools around the country will provide protective clothing, a racing machine and expert guidance and tuition. If you want to be an 'instant' road racer, why not try your hand with them? The Dixon Racing School is one of these organisations. Some of Britain's top riders act as its instructors. The schools offer a cheap way of finding out if you could perhaps become Britain's next Mike Hailwood, without the head-aches.

And if you find that racing isn't for you, I know just the place to buy a good set of second-hand golf clubs!

CHAPTER 4

World championship trail

by Rod Gould, 1970 250 cc world champion and Yamaha
publicity manager for Europe

IT'S ONLY WHEN you lose something that you realise how much it means to you. In 1970, after I had had the good fortune to become the 250 cc world champion, it was all really a bit of an anti-climax. Ever since I had started racing in 1961 my target had been to become a world champion, although at first I hadn't realised this. And the season I finally made it, everything had been geared towards that aim. So when the title was clinched I just didn't feel any different, although naturally I was pleased at winning the championship.

But I can tell you I felt very unhappy the following year to lose it. The sudden realisation that you are no longer the champ takes a lot of swallowing. Anyone who says that the world championships mean nothing to a rider does not know what it feels like to suddenly not be world champion. Not that the world championship trail is everyone's ideal form of racing. There are many good riders, John Cooper and Derek Minter, for example, who have never been interested in contesting the GP series. Just because I raced in GP events it does not mean to say that they are the best thing going in motorcycle sport. They just happen to be the type of racing I prefer. Both Cooper and Minter became very successful in the sphere in which they decided to specialise, ie short circuit racing. And you cannot knock them, and other riders like them, for that. They reached the top of the tree for which they were aiming.

There is a great deal of difference in riding techniques for short circuit and grand prix racing. Short circuit racing is the best possible training for a rider who wants to chase world championships, that's for sure. From the drop of the flag you have to go all out for 10 or 15 laps—there's no let-up. And though in the GPs the pace is perhaps a little slower because you need to maintain it for a longer period of time, it's easier for a 'scratcher' to become a successful GP rider, than for a so-called polished or stylish rider to turn scratcher and still win. If you are a good short circuit rider it is easier to slow down and learn to pace yourself. But if you start in GPs before you reach the top of short circuit racing, you'll never know how fast you can go. This has happened to a lot of riders. They've moved on to world championship races too soon. They start in GPs without mastering short circuit-type all-action stuff, and they never learn how to scratch.

There are some riders who are great at the Isle of Man once a year. Then they fade into obscurity for 364 days. But other well known riders can also win at the TT, go to Mallory the following week, win there, and move on to a Continental GP seven days later and win there too! You can judge for yourself who is the better rider.

One of the reasons British and Commonwealth riders have enjoyed so much success in the past is that there are so many race meetings in Britain to sharpen up a rider before he moves on to bigger things. On the Continent there used to be fewer events, and so our boys held the advantage. But now, as the number of road race meetings increases abroad, foreign riders have started to master both styles of riding. Finland's 250 cc world champion, Jarno Saarinen, is a perfect example. After a brilliant GP season in 1972, he came to Mallory Park and won the Rothmans 'Race of the Year', which featured the most costly line-up of riders ever presented at a British meeting.

But while the GPs and the short circuits demand differing techniques and strategies, a rider's style must remain identical for both sports. Paul Smart uses his famous 'knee-out' style whether he is on a British short circuit, in a GP, or contesting a 200-mile Formula 750 marathon. The best style is the one which enables you to go the quickest. It's fatal to purposely attempt to adopt someone else's style. People try to copy Paul, they have tried to copy Agostini and Geoff Duke, and way back no doubt they even imitated Edgar Jessop. It's all a waste of time. The best style is the one that comes naturally to you, because you'll go faster using it.

Tactics, however, must vary between short circuits and GP racing. On many of the GP circuits you can't ride as though you were at Brands Hatch. You need to pace yourself.

In the TT races there is one perennial hero—the 37¾-mile Mountain circuit. Here its moors and mists loom over Rod Gould, as he races the works Yamaha to second place in the 1972 250 cc event.

The last lap has to be ridden as fast as the first lap, and to try to ride at eleven tenths, something you could perhaps get away with in a 15-lap short circuit event, is asking for trouble over the longer distances and different circuits involved in the world championships.

Sometimes it is possible to win races by setting such a cracking pace at the start that you break completely away from the field. If there are no fighters among the opposition, the field will just give up and let you go. Even if they don't, the theory is that you can afford to slow down once your lead is established, and they still won't have time to catch you. I tried this at the Swedish GP at Anderstorp in 1972. In the 500 cc race I realised the only chance of beating Agostini was to go flat-out from the fall of the flag and build up a big lead. His MV was faster than my Yamaha, but I still hoped that he wouldn't be able to catch me. After five laps I'd opened up a 13-second lead. But on the fourteenth lap, even though I had not slowed at all, the MV passed me, and it was impossible for me to carry on at the sort of pace I had set. It was a case of the straight being a little bit too long, and the MV was able to outpace my Yamaha.

But these tactics did work once, and again it was with Agostini. The race was one I shall never forget—the Post-TT meeting at Mallory in 1969. It was just 20 laps long, and I had decided that my only chance was to try to make the break right from the start and hope Agostini would be caught on the hop. He wasn't expecting it, and that worked in my favour. On my 350 cc Yamaha I opened a gap, and I was still in front at the flag—only by 0.6 seconds, but it was enough to make me the first privateer to beat Agostini.

Looking every inch the professional, Rod Gould sweeps round Brands Hatch in 1969, one of his most successful years on British circuits.

Championship year: Rod Gould leads Kel Carruthers at Wheelers Corner during the 250 cc race at the 1970 Ulster GP. Rod went on to take the 250 cc world title.

Judging the pace is perhaps the most difficult task in GP racing, and the world champions are those who can assess it best. It's not easy to tell how quickly the rest are going, even after practice. I know I'm not the only one who could go faster in the race than in training. I used to tell myself that practice was only practice. But there are riders, like Phil Read, for example, who can go just as quickly in practice as in the race. If at the close of the practice periods you see that you are half a second slower than another rider, you have to know if he is someone who, perhaps like you, can quicken his pace in the race, or not. Most riders can. At some short circuit type GP tracks, like Anderstorp, it may be possible to take one second off your practice time, but that's all. In the Isle of Man you can chop perhaps 30 or 40 seconds off a lap. Jarno Saarinen is a rider who can always go faster in the race than he does in practice, and he has a habit of going quickly in practice, too!

Determination and dedication are other key factors in the making of a world champion. A good GP rider wants to succeed. Unless you are at the top, world championship racing is a poorly paid business. You must have the will to win, and whether it's actually possible for you to win or not doesn't really matter.

You must be sure that your machine is the best available to you in the circumstances, and you must be organised. Sometimes the FIM link five or six GPs together on consecutive weekends. Consequently, if your machines, your transport, your entries and paper-work are not properly arranged, the trouble you'll find yourself in and the time you waste can be staggering.

If you have bad luck, you have to shrug it off. It's happened, and you can't undo it. If you break down on the last lap of a 100-mile race, there is no point in getting de-tuned about it. Just make sure, if possible, that it doesn't happen again.

There is plenty of hard scenery around most GP circuits, and you must bear that in mind, too. That's not to say you take it easy. You ride hard. But though you may race at eleven tenths on a British short circuit, you only ride at nine or nine-and-a-half, occasionally at ten tenths, at a GP.

Your relationships with fellow competitors tend to be rather different on the GP trail. If you spend most of your time travelling, eating and talking together, then when there is room for only one rider to go through at a corner, and he has a slight advantage, you back off and let him go. Don't try and push him off. It only causes a lot of bad feeling. A good rider will always back off if the alternative looks like turning into an accident. A bad rider

The rivals: Rod Gould and Phil Read, who fought for the 250 cc world championship in 1971, stage a minibike burn-up, refereed by Ray Pickrell.

will press through. It may look as though the man who has forced through has come out on top, but really he hasn't. The man who gave way and prevented both riders from crashing has used his head and is the best rider. In my experience, the man who eases off when it seems the right thing to do will usually pass his wilder opponent later in the race anyway.

Nobby Clarke, the Rhodesian mechanic who has worked with many top liners, including Mike Hailwood and Gary Hocking, over the past decade, was once asked what was the quality that was common to all the great riders he had known.

'They wanted to be the best in everything they did,' was his reply.

If the sort of people who make world champions cannot be the best, they will either not take up a particular activity, or they will keep practising until they reach the top. If you are prepared to take second best at one thing, you'll be ready to accept second best, or second place, in another sphere—and you'll never become a world champion like that. Dedication is the keynote. Obviously, you cannot be the best at everything, but you can go down trying. It's not riding style that matters, but mental attitude. Do not accept second best! Of present-day riders, Barry Sheene has this quality. He isn't interested in second and third places; he wants to be first. And if he wants it badly enough, he can become a future world champion for Britain. Yorkshire's Mick Grant is perhaps the best of the up-and-coming British hopes at the moment, but I don't know him well enough to say if he has the necessary will to win that could carry him right to the top. But I hope he's got it, because I feel that at present there are very few British riders on the way up who look potential world champions.

I'm not saying that there is no riding talent about. But the high costs of racing, the limited amount of sponsorship available, and increased competition from abroad make things so much harder for British riders who are keen to make the grade.

It's this will to win that I keep talking about that really is the key to success. People say

Rod Gould gets his Yamaha off the grid ahead of Giacomo Agostini (MV), Phil Read (Yamaha, 8) and Kel Carruthers (Yamaha, 3) at the 350 cc race of the Dutch TT.

that works bikes enable factory-supported riders to win, and though that may be true of some exotic machines, it doesn't apply to Yamaha's factory racers. The 'works' Yamahas are very similar to the production machines that anyone can buy. They incorporate a few modifications for development purposes, and their water cooling does aid performance by about 10 per cent, but that isn't really so much. In any case, the 'special' parts are more often than not incorporated into the following year's production machines. The 1972 water-cooled factory bikes are now Yamaha's production racing models.

The 1972 Yamaha factory team was a big one—too big, as it turned out, and I'm sure that the company will not repeat the mistake. It was made up of six riders—five Europeans and a Japanese. Each rider used one water-cooled machine as his number one bike, and was also given an air-cooled model of a different capacity so that he could support riders with the water-cooled machines in another class. Kent Andersson and Charles Mortimer had water-cooled 125s, Barry Sheene and myself ran water-cooled 250s (initially, at least), and Jarno Saarinen and Hideo Kanaya used water-cooled 350s. Andersson, Mortimer, Saarinen and Kanaya rode air-cooled 250s, to start with, to back up Barry Sheene and myself, while Barry and I rode air-cooled bikes in the 350 cc class to aid Jarno and Hideo. Complicated!

Kanaya only raced in Europe until the Belgian GP before returning home, though while he was here he rode to really good effect. Barry, of course, had an accident in the Italian GP that put him out of action for some weeks. This left spare 250 and 350 cc water-cooled bikes. As Saarinen was going so well in the 250 cc class, the factory decided to let him have the 250. It was a move that certainly paid off, because Jarno went on to win the world title for that class. The water-cooled 350 was put into storage until Barry had recovered. Charles Mortimer and I had no inclination to use it, as we had both moved on to the 500 cc class to test experimental air-cooled 352 cc barrels against the Suzukis, Kawasakis, Konigs, Lintos and MVs. There were no team orders, or a team manager. If it looked a little disorganised to anyone on the outside, that was probably because it was a little chaotic. But we got results, although they could have been better.

Although there isn't much advantage in being a works rider as far as performance goes, there are financial benefits. It costs a privateer about £5,000 to set himself up properly for a serious world championship bid, so the works riders enjoy a useful 'bonus' before they have even raced. Factory payments today are not as high as when Yamaha were racing in the mid-'sixties with Phil Read and the late Bill Ivy, but every rider does get a signing-on fee, which varies from man to man. There are no bonuses, and the contract is for just one year. But it is a lot easier to seek benefits from the few trade people who still support racing if you are a factory-backed rider. It is perhaps a sad irony that the people who are just starting and who need the help most, cannot get it and the riders at the top receive the extra trade boosts. But the trade just cannot afford to risk backing a potential loser, and while there are no certainties in racing, factory support usually means winners. And that's what a sponsor of any sort wants.

A further advantage to being a factory rider is that it's usually easier to negotiate with organisers for start money. But this doesn't always work. Some GP organisers reason that works riders must attend GPs on company orders. They then offer minimal financial terms. As far as Yamaha are concerned, this ruling applies to every GP except one. The exception is the TT. Yamaha say they would prefer to race there, but the final decision rests with the riders, although they did veto Kanaya's TT entry outright in 1972. As he was a complete newcomer to the GP scene, they considered the event was just too dangerous for him.

Most people do not realise that it is thanks to Yamaha's European head office in Holland that the company is still in racing today. In 1968 the head office in Japan issued clear instructions: no more racing. But in 1970 the company's European officials decided to race

Learn to ride hard on home circuits before you race abroad, Rod Gould advises. Here, on his Norton in 1967, he's doing just that, in a battle with Matchless-mounted Ron Chandler (2) and the late John Hartle (8). The event is a 500 cc final at Mallory Park.

on a limited scale with just Kent Andersson and myself. We were successful—that was the year I won my 250 cc world title—and the factory's top brass in Japan were pleased. It was agreed that the European organisation could continue racing, but on a small scale, primarily to test parts for later production models. That is really the reason that our 1971 season was not so happy. We were experimenting for much of the time, and that, coupled with some bad luck, spoilt the year.

Yamaha race, both in road racing and in moto cross, for development and publicity, with the emphasis on publicity. They, too, have the will to win. Second place is no good to them. Just look at their motto: 'Yamaha—it's a better machine'. Before that it was 'Yamaha—World Champion'. They figure that if you are going to do something, be the best at it, or don't do it at all.

Publicity, then, is of paramount importance. But people who ride Yamahas on the road also feel the benefit of race track testing. The company's 250 and 350 cc road machines use the frame from the GP racers. The crankcase and crankshaft on the road machines come directly from the TR3 racers. There are not many factories who do that!

Since the major Japanese factories pulled out of racing in the late 'sixties, there has been a feeling that world championship events are now 'easy'. I think this attitude is without foundation. The world championships may have lost some of their glamour at that time, but to say that the classics suddenly became easier to win is rubbish. You have to ride just as hard to win on a 50 bhp machine, as on an 80 bhp model, if all other riders are similarly mounted.

The Japanese factories pulled out in 1968 when the FIM limited GP road racing machines to two cylinders and six-speed gearboxes. With those limits on design, Yamaha and Honda said, 'We can learn nothing'. There is no point in racing if it does not aid development. And with production racers able to win for them at national level, they did not need GP success for publicity. The fact that after Honda withdrew from racing, the proposed restrictions on multi-cylinder 350s and 500s were lifted, may have escaped some people's notice. Now moto cross seems to be going the same way. Newly introduced minimum weight restrictions and limitations on the choice of materials appear to favour European factories.

When the FIM change of rules caused the exotic Japanese GP machines to go into

Sight-seeing: Jarno Saarinen and his wife Soeli take a trip round the Silverstone paddock. Saarinen was Yamaha's most successful rider in 1972, winning the 250 cc world title.

retirement, the factories' giant publicity and advertising departments were also lost to the sport. Crowds decreased, although in recent years attendances have started to climb again. But whatever decline there has been can still be laid firmly at the feet of the FIM. If the major Japanese factories were all still racing, motorcycle GPs would be as highly publicised as Formula 1 car racing.

Formula 750 could still do this for motorcycle sport. But unless race organisers cease to merely add the new class to existing race programmes, treating it as just another part of the day's events, then it will not survive. The experimental Formula 750 race at the 1972 Swedish GP was the first time that the new class had been catered for at a Continental classic. But it was a flop. Formula 750 deserves a big build-up, but in Sweden, and at the Silverstone international in Britain, it was just one of many races. It wasn't even the fastest, either, which it must be if it is to be taken seriously by the crowds.

And when all is said and done it's spectators that count. As a former professional rider— now retired—and a Yamaha employee, I considered the number of people who watched me and the rest of the boys race, and who then bought their motorcycles on the basis of our success, to be of the umost importance.

I have always been amazed at the rather peculiar attitude that many British riders tend to adopt when they first break into Continental racing. No matter how successful they have been in England, they are worth no more to a foreign organiser than anyone else making his first appearance at that track. Their value is based solely on how many spectators they attract. If more riders looked on their first year's racing abroad as an investment for the future they would do much better for themselves. They might take three years to establish their reputation, but if they do the job properly they will make ten-fold the money they 'lost' in the early years. To say you must never race for low start money is rubbish. At the start of your career you have to. If you ride to the best of your ability, run the most competitive machinery you can afford, and try your utmost to finish, you will soon be working well with the organisers. And when that happens you can start to make your racing pay.

Too many riders want to make a one-sided deal. But it is in everybody's interest for organisers and riders to work together to provide a decent show. If the organisers want you to help with some additional job, then why not? You could win more fans, and the race could attract more spectators.

Not every race is won in the workshop or on the track. It is possible to talk your way to victory. Phil Read is perhaps the best of the present-day 'psychological warfare' men. Everyone does it a bit, but Phil is an expert. In 1971 he took the 250 cc world title from me. I don't put that down to his 'brainwashing' abilities—but, boy, did he try! It became something of a paddock joke. You would see Phil wandering round the riders, and if he happened to visit Barry Sheene before me, Barry would pop round to say: 'Phil's on his rounds again'. I would then warn Barry if Phil had made me his first call. 'Bit slippery on such and such a corner,' Phil would say in casual conversation, or, 'It looks a bit like rain'. I'm sure it doesn't work on me, but I do know riders who are affected by such tactics.

It's not just the things you say that can help win the battle of the minds. Sometimes it's simply enough to appear better off financially, or just to have a mechanic to assist you. Even a bit of secrecy on routine maintenance can give the impression that you are using special parts. And an air of 'quiet confidence' can sometimes send a rival away thinking, 'I'm sure there's nothing to his confidence, but maybe . . .' And once the seed of doubt is sown, you can often reap a rich harvest.

Even with practice times a little bit of 'conning' can help. In a restaurant after practice at one GP, Phil and I were casually chatting about lap times. 'How did you go', he asked me, 'I don't really know what sort of times I managed'. I told him he'd recorded a time some ten seconds slower than the lap which had actually put him at the top of the day's practice.

'I didn't,' said Phil indignantly, 'I did a three minutes eighteen seconds!'

The cheeky blighter had known all along! On that occasion I caught him out, but I wonder how often before then he'd been stringing me along?

Sometimes, though, the war of nerves between Phil and myself in the closely contested 250 cc battle of 1971 actually upset everyone else except us two. At the East German GP that year, as we waited to go on to the grid, Phil pointed out a trail of cement dust that indicated oil. It was right on the fastest line at the tricky uphill left hander before the finish. Phil claimed that this line of oil had been dropped on the track for nearly half the circuit, including the very fast downhill section towards the grandstands. Sportingly, it seemed, he was putting me in the picture. But when I sent my mechanic to check with the riders in the 125 cc race, that had just ended, it became clear that the oil was confined to one small stretch of the circuit. The effect of Phil's 'traffic report' on the rest of the competitors was devastating, because when we came to the first corner at which he had

The 250 cc water-cooled engine that won the 1972 world championship for Yamaha. Bore and stroke are 54 × 54 mm, and maximum power is about 60 bhp.

alleged the oil started, everybody except Phil and I slowed down dramatically. We opened up a 150-yard lead over the others before they realised they had been 'had'.

How long this sort of psychological warfare has been going on I don't know. But Phil must have learnt it somewhere! Even in Britain, I have been able to con a few riders. When I used to race my 250 cc Bultaco-framed Yamaha I used to really have to struggle at times with other guys, until I would make a supreme effort round one corner, and then 'casually' glance back to see where the others were. More often than not, they would then say to themselves, 'Let's settle for an easy second'. What they didn't know was that if they had carried on pressing me they would probably have won. Some people say you need luck to win races, but that sort of thing helps you to make your own luck.

The turning point in my racing life wasn't really luck, either. It came with a trip to America in 1967 with Bruce Cox, an old friend of mine who later returned to the States to run *Motor Cycle Weekly*, which is now the biggest-selling motorcycle newspaper in the USA. We both needed a 'lucky' break. My 350 and 500 cc Nortons were not quick enough to win GPs any more, and Bruce had tried one or two business ventures that had not worked. California appeared to be where it was all at, for both business and racing opportunities. So we went. It was from that trip that I was able to do the groundwork that enabled me to bring back to this country a Yamaha TD1C motor that certainly gave me the break I needed in my racing career. The trip blew all our combined savings, but it was worth it. We came back to this country with me having an engine and no money, and Bruce evolving an idea for a newspaper, and no money! I think it worked for both of us. Never complain about anyone having a 'lucky' break. More often than not, that break had to be earned the hard way.

*Chas Mortimer, pictured here on the 125 **Yamaha**, has won **two** 125 cc TTs for the factory.*

CHAPTER 5

Angle on promotion

by Jim Swift, circuit manager, Mallory Park, and former secretary of the British Motor Cycle Racing Club

---

IF ROAD RACING was run for horses instead of motorcycles, then the sport would be a lot better off than it is right now. Come to think of it we would all be a lot better off: riders, promoters and organisers. But it isn't, and we have to suffer the humiliation of being a huge sport without the recognition we so justly deserve. How many of us have whined at the complete disinterest of the mass media at the time of the TT? How many of us have switched on the radio to catch a brief report only to find that because our watches were a few seconds out we have missed it? Road racing is an important part of this country's sporting successes dating way back to Brooklands in 1907 and even before. Why then should it prove to be of so little interest until fatalities and crashes force it into the headlines?

Angling is the world's largest participation sport; soccer is the world's largest spectator sport. Where road racing comes between the two I don't know, but it must certainly rate higher than show jumping, golf and athletics. No doubt some genius will work out that the British Open produced a fantastic crowd this year at Muirfield, but then so did the TT and certainly every European GP produces crowds in excess of golfing figures. But road racing does suffer from a lack of personalities. It hasn't a Harvey Smith or a Dave Bedford to its name and it is still dubbed in some quarters as a dirty, smelly, noisy sport—which in some respects it is, of course.

But the trouble is a lot more fundamental. Motorcycling has a bad image dating back to the days when the minority element used an otherwise highly efficient mode of transport as a platform for gang warfare. Leather jackets, coarse speech and noisy machines were so portrayed by films, television presentations and the newspapers as to suggest that motorcycling was nothing else. Many organisations tried to change the image, with a small amount of success, but it was a mere drop in the ocean compared with the damage already done. And it was into the ocean that the motorcycling movement would like to have dropped the more sensational reports!

Promotion, they say, is the art of persuading the public into doing something they had never considered. In theory this is quite plausible, but somehow it just doesn't work in road racing. I suppose the reason is simply the fact that there is no fringe element; either you like motorcycle racing or you don't, and the only attraction which will decide you for or against is the quality of the entry. Man's own human endeavours have always appealed more to the public at large than when he has machine assistance. People who have no real interest in cricket go along just for a day out. People go to Wimbledon because it is the done thing and, if you like, television has given them the chance to see what it's all about beforehand. It's clean, white and—beyond all else—it's quiet!

Promoters today are faced with ever rising prices; in fact the same battle that society as a whole faces from day to day. The manufactured product is entertainment out of doors which in any country is a hazardous pastime except, perhaps, somewhere like California where they have never heard of tinned strawberries! In this fair land of ours the weather is totally unpredictable, the risks of failure disproportionately high, and only a fool would try to run an event at the beginning of March or in mid-November. Promoters are not fools, however, but then we have had some really superb weather in March and November which somehow makes the risk that little more acceptable.

Saturday race meetings are now almost a thing of the past. They disappeared when supermarkets were introduced. Where is the point of running a Saturday fixture when you know for a fact that Saturday, to the vast majority, is the first opportunity to do the shopping, to service the car when the garages are open for spares, and when the motorcycle trade is at its busiest? So we go road racing on a Sunday, but not on any Sunday.

Quite often I sit back and wonder where this sport of ours is heading. For years now it seems to have been erupting in one way or another and the politics and battles become increasingly tiring as the years unfold. As in all sports it is governed by an international organisation—and therein lies its major problems. The needs of the sport vary from country to country and from year to year, but an organisation which is so huge as to encompass the world is very slow to recognise change and even slower to help that change along. What a promoter could achieve in a month will take such a political body at least a year and possibly even longer. Put the world's promoters together and it will happen overnight.

The fundamental difference is that the promoter is motivated along a more selective line. Whereas the international organisation has only the sport at heart, the promoter has both the sport and the profit motive to drive him along much faster. He is good for the sport since he, and he alone, can inject the capital, provide the circuits and facilities, and soak up the obvious financial losses which the sport and the governing bodies could not possibly bear. Not all promotions are successful, and the year has to be taken as a whole, although obviously no promoter wants to repeat a calamity. When he makes a profit a percentage goes to the governing body. Even when he applies for a date he pays a fee, so without the promoter the sport would be almost non-existent. Race meetings don't just happen, they are created—often 12 months ahead of the scheduled date. Many people scheme and work to better the sport, to bring originality and spectacle into the lives of the average motorcycle enthusiast, and without them I hate to think what the future would be.

The average spectator knows exactly what he wants to see. If the local cinema puts on a bad film the box office sales are low; it's just the same in any sport and motorcycle racing is no exception. Correspondingly, a good film costs more to rent and the admission charges rise proportionately. A first-class international entry at a race meeting is very expensive and the admission charge must reflect the risk involved. Far from being the evil profiteer, as the general promoter is dubbed, the costs and pitfalls of present-day promotion are tremendously risky and, like any successful business, the year must be taken as a whole. In effect this means that every activity goes to make up the balance sheet and even the most successful of motorcycle races eventually go to balance out the worst of car races, and vice versa of course.

Therefore, the spectator must expect to pay a reasonable admission fee for all types of meeting, this fee being determined by the costs involved in putting on the event. Only the promoter knows what these costs are and it is useless for anyone else to try and guess them. Who else knows what proportion rates, salaries and maintenance make in the calculation?

Promoters in Britain have been quick to encourage the exciting spectacle offered by F750 machinery. Here, during the 1972 Race of the Year meeting at Mallory Park, John Cooper (1) and Ray Pickrell (Triumph-3s) lead Paul Smart (6, Seeley-Kawasaki), Tony Jefferies (11, Triumph-3), Dave Potter (42, Kuhn Norton), Mick Grant (16, John Player Norton), and Bob Heath (27, BSA twin).

One of Motor Circuit Developments' greatest successes was in introducing Cal Rayborn to Britain for the 1972 John Player Transatlantic Trophy series at Brands, Mallory and Oulton. Rayborn (right) responded by winning three of the rounds, and Britain's Ray Pickrell (left) won the remaining three. Between them is Rayborn's mechanic Walt Faulk.

Who else knows how much the police services cost and the hundred and one other hidden factors behind even the smallest meeting? Who else knows the total prize and appearance money bill, and that it has to be met in full even if it tipples down with rain all day and keeps most spectators away? Who else but the person who is laying out the hard capital?

Road racing is business through and through: from the FIM through the ACU (the governing bodies), through the promoters and the organising clubs, whether the latter like to admit it or not. The cool hard fact is that unless you can make money you cannot speculate, and when you are unable to do so then you reach the position of stagnation. The sport cannot go forward without someone taking risks and a wise man risks only that which he can afford to lose.

To my mind motorcycle racing is the finest sport in the world. The professional and amateur mix amicably and compete side by side. There are no throat-cutting politics which despoil it in the eyes of the world, and whereas it tends to suffer from its own particular problems, it maintains a permanent stature regardless of all other influences. If anything it is gradually growing out of the doldrums a new body which certainly augurs well for the future.

Its biggest problem today is that of safety. We all know that road racing is a dangerous sport, and the more we are reminded about it the better. A complete awareness of the danger is absolutely necessary both from the riders' and the spectators' points of view because without it people become a danger to themselves, and when they become that they also become a danger to everyone else. The changing face of the world's circuits is a tremendous problem for the riders, who become more and more aware that what is safe for the car drivers is spelling more danger to themselves. Crash barriers, designed to slide the cars to safety and to protect the spectator, are a tremendous hazard, for the motorcyclist isn't protected by a metal shroud and the flimsy body inside a suit of leather doesn't stand much of a chance against tensioned steel and three inch wooden walls. The basic requirements of the two forms of motoring sport are vastly different. Some idealists are trying to say that a circuit should be used for motorcycle racing or car racing only and that the two should not run on the same circuit. While one would never dream of faulting this rather bold idea, given the choice there are few promoters who would favour motorcycling; which would in effect mean that the sport would dwindle into obscurity with perhaps the small circuit owner with the lesser overheads and operation costs laughing all the way to the bank. Spectators enjoy variety and I don't believe that, given a choice of only a few circuits, their enthusiasm would last all that long.

The only alternative is co-existence. But since the two governing bodies of motor and motorcycle racing are a world apart, due to the completely differing nature of their requirements, that co-existence rests on the flimsiest of objectives. Where there are crash barriers it is sensible to suggest that there should be something softer in front of them for motorcycle meetings. Having explored the alternatives of padding, the only readily available economical suggestion is straw baling. But bales have to be stored from one harvest to the next and deteriorate through use. If you start off with 3,000 bales you may need another 2,000 before the season ends. Handling bales (which are hardly ever wired these days but combined with rot-proof string) wrecks the vast majority, particularly as they have to be removed from the circuit every time a car meeting is run. Although the problems are being examined, answers are slow to appear, for foam blocks are tremendously expensive. Whereas a Continental organiser may run one major event a year, a British promoter wants something that must be capable of withstanding continuous use in all climatic conditions.

Some promoters now enjoy claiming their support of motorcycle racing by announcing their objections to the car safety regulations, which gives the appearance that some circuits are more pro-motorcycles than others. Although this may well be a genuine feeling, it doesn't alter the fact that every racing circuit in the world that wants to run both forms of sport has to do something about the plight of the motorcyclist, either from the dictates of the governing body of sport in their country, or if not, from the demands of the riders. Some circuits are more adversely affected than others, and it rather depends upon the nature of the circuit as to whether or not the expense is great or small. And one must remember that, to complicate things still further, some European promoters don't even approve of the car safety regulations!

It is beyond the ability of the average spectator to comprehend the complexities of circuit management and, although we all stand to be criticised from time to time, the fundamental aspects of racing are much too involved to be readily explainable. Most British circuits have grown with the sport, and unlike their European and American counterparts which have provided planned facilities at an enormous initial outlay, most have progressed steadily from post-war airfields or from grass tracks. The Japanese and American race circuits are carefully planned business enterprises that encompass trade and industrial development, which is perhaps the major objective. The relatively cheap cost and the availability of land, not to mention the more readily available capital in such expanding industrial countries, makes this type of project sensible and justifiable.

In Europe this is not entirely the case as the major circuits have been around for an awfully long time now, although circuits like Avus (now no longer used) opened with the need of Mercedes and Auto Union to have a private test ground. The Japanese circuit of Suzuka was built by Honda for Honda and because it cost anyone else a fortune to use, the Japanese built Fuji outside Tokyo. The Paul Ricard circuit in the South of France is one of the newest enterprises, but even that has enormous trade backing, and with its siting in the more sunny and forceful areas of French economical life it should, in theory, prove most successful.

At a time when expansion is needed, when money could be available for new schemes, more and more is being spent on basic safety protection, on fire fighting equipment, on medical aspects. New rules instigated by the governing bodies mean that less expansion is possible at a time when the sport needs it, and could react to it best. Circuit improvements are held up and the spectator, who basically only wants to see good racing, is caught up in the political exchanges.

There are basically three types of meeting run in this country—international, national and club level events. All three require promoting and only the latter may be treated as pure sport from the monetary angle, since it may derive all or part of its promotional costs from entry fees which the competitors pay. With the ever-increasing costs of printing and circuit hire, it is very unlikely that any organising club can do without even minimal support from the spectator, who must be wooed with advertising. Club racing can be good fun for the competitor and a cheap and enjoyable day's viewing for those who take the trouble to pay to watch. The spectator has no need to bother too much with his programme since the standard of competition is excellent, everyone being as good as each other if the races are graded correctly. There are no firm favourites, so it doesn't matter much who wins.

The stakes at national level are higher. To justify its continued inclusion in the calendar the promoter must see to it that this type of meeting produces the crowds, although his objectives are tempered with the knowledge that it is always unwise to spend too much in an attempt to produce a fat income. Those days have long since passed and nowadays he is looking for a more modest return.

Huge crowds can only be drawn to the big internationals, since it is apparent that, in general, spectators only want to see the big stars. Allied to this is the unfortunate fact that these stars want rather a lot of money to compete, which tends to put the ordinary national event outside the realms of possibility. Only at certain times of the year can a national event boast an above-average entry, when the date in the calendar is favourable and when the promoter is blessed with a round of a popular championship. Even then he will think more than once before putting too much at risk, as even the most favourable national event has been known to misfire rather badly.

International events are a different kettle of fish entirely since one can appeal to the foreign riders and thence produce the world champions and riders who normally are seldom seen in England. The expense is tremendous and the stars' appearance can run the promoter into laying out many thousands of pounds. International dates have to be slotted into the international calendar as the movement of the stars necessarily falls into the routine of the world championships. With 13 world championship rounds in 1972, all of them designed, it seemed, to produce the most tiring mileage, competitors had little time to themselves; little time to repair broken machinery and, above all, little time to look after their own private business of negotiation with organisers of non-world championship events. The struggle to keep up with them is becoming more tedious but it is a very necessary part of this by now misused of all words—promotion. But how often do pro-

What was it like to ride the 107 bhp water-cooled Suzukis in the 1972 Transatlantic series?
'Pretty freaky,' Ron Grant (left) seems to think, while team-mate Art Baumann makes sure
he still has a head.

moters claim the attendance of a particular rider only to find out at the last minute that he cannot turn out? By and large you can blame the world championship rounds since their close proximity to each other means that there is no time to replace machinery, and with the continuous run of events personal injury also remains a high factor which no one, least of all the competitor, can foresee.

When race day dawns it is very much an anti-climax for the promoter and a climax for the spectator—which is just what any good promotion should be. By now the publicity has gone out and people have been told who is going to be where and at what time. The better the meeting the better the publicity, particularly at international events which, in themselves, generate their own publicity. The sun may be shining or it may be teeming with rain. A risk has been taken and it has either been worth it or it hasn't. Next week another event . . . and another carefully planned enterprise. It may be cars, it may be bikes or it may even be a caravan rally, in which case the spectator looks to another circuit and another promoter to supply him with what he wants most that particular weekend. Perhaps even the traction engine rally out at Specton-under-Sea appeals to him more than a national, in which case the choice is entirely his. Spectators don't have to go and watch motorcycle racing, but it is the promoter's task to attract them.

Within this closely controlled arena comes another category of person who plays a very important part—the sponsor. Whether it be Castrol or one of the tobacco giants, the infiltration of promotional capital is necessary if one is to maintain a continuity of purpose. The creation of championships for types and classes of racing is a priority since it cements the average spectator to a series of races throughout the country, the progress of which he can follow through the technical press or personally at his own favourite circuit.

Secondly, the sponsor's capital is necessary to broaden the scope of racing; to put on something different when the average promoter cannot himself justify the complete capital expense. This is not to suggest that the sponsor acts as a buffer that the promoter can hide behind in case of emergency, but more that the two interested parties can collectively decide upon a promotion which suits them both, knowing the risks and problems involved.

For his money, the sponsor needs publicity and the more the better, which suits the promoter well as his interests are obviously the same. Recently in motor racing and again in motorcycle racing we have seen a slight change in direction. Tobacco firms that have been stopped from advertising through the TV channels have fortunately diverted part of their budgets to motor and motorcycle racing. Cricket, football and many other sports have also benefited from more money being available.

During recent years a lot has been written about the poor association between riders and promoters. Most of it is nothing short of sensationalism conjured up at a time of year when there is little else to write about. I'm not pretending that everything in the cabbage patch is entirely without grubs, but if you dig around long enough you are bound to find something. The changing face of professionalism within motorcycle sport has not been without its teething troubles. Although the professional rider at the height of the Japanese monopoly in the 'sixties was asking (and getting) quite a sizeable chunk of the meat, he was at least riding the finest machines in the world maintained in perfect condition and guaranteed to give of their best. It was money well spent. When the Japanese pulled out of racing these riders were left with ex-works machines which became increasingly unreliable, and since the cost of keeping them running at all became proportionately expensive, their claims rose until either they wore out their own welcome, or their machinery fell apart, in which case the net result was the same.

These were the days when the struggle between promoter and rider was at its height. They were closely followed by a new spate of private enterprise, in which the arguments were to re-emerge as demands for riches comparable with those earned in the halcyon days. Costs had risen, riders had to buy their own machines, provide their own mechanics and cover their own expenses. If promoters were to agree to these sudden increased costs, the cost to the public would be higher and for this reason as much as any other negotiations were often quite lengthy. Small wonder, therefore, that some riders felt slighted and rushed their complaints to the nearest pressman, who accepted the gossip as only a journalist would.

Negotiations today are equally hard, but on the whole I believe that tempers have settled down and riders, organisers and promoters work more closely together. Colour and spectacle have replaced the traditionally drab, black scene, and the manufacturer, particularly the British manufacturer, has suddenly found new life and success. A new arena for competition has been created in that the United States has been brought into the world motorcycling scene; a new Superbike class has been created and now the FIM are being persuaded to create a new world championship.

Creation is the heart and sole of promotion. When creation fails, promotion, and thence the sport, drifts aimlessly until someone picks up the pieces!

CHAPTER 6

A world-beater from a roadster

by Doug Hele, Chief Development Engineer,
Triumph Engineering Co Ltd

IF FORMULA 750 is the spectacle which has revived road racing after some of the duller years of the late '60s, I believe that the 750 cc Triumph and BSA three-cylinder models are largely responsible for the initial success of the class. We were among the first factories to build machines specifically for F750 racing, and certainly we were the very first European manufacturer to do so. Our bikes went on to become the most successful machines in the Formula. For the first time in 20 years, British motorcycles led the world in international road racing, a thrilling prospect for the thousands of enthusiasts who had become used to seeing great British riders winning, but invariably on Japanese or Continental machinery.

Without our presence, F750 would still have become the prestige class in road racing; but I think it's no exaggeration to say that the process would have been much slower. The sight and the sound of the 'threes' in action on the world's major circuits won us immense publicity, and gave our opposition a target to aim at. Without that, technical development in F750 would not have been as rapid, and the class would not have commanded such immediate respect.

The 'threes' have their origin back in 1963, when two basic factors brought Mr Bert Hopwood, who was then Triumph's director and general manager, and I to the conclusion that the concept of a 750 cc three-cylinder four-stroke should receive some exploration. One fact was that the 650 cc twin-cylinder Triumph engine, even in unit construction form, was not an easy engine to make smooth. Secondly, the 750 cc Norton Atlas engine of that time, which we had developed while previously working at Nortons, ran much rougher than its 650 cc counterpart. Such facts are not surprising, but they did indicate that for a 750 cc machine, a different design than a parallel twin was necessary.

The exercise of designing and developing a 'three' really started in 1964, and the first engine ran on the test bench on January 12 1965. But since few other people in the company, particularly at top level, were interested in its progress, the flow of components was rather slow, and budget expenditure on the project was kept to a minimum.

The first conception called for an ohv engine with a bore and stroke of 63 × 80 mm, and boasted primary drive by three gears, and an oil pump mounted beneath the engine and driven by a skew gear from the inlet camshaft. The cylinder barrel was cast iron. The first engine on the test bench was soon giving an acceptable 59 bhp at 8,000 rpm, fitted with silencers.

Two views at Devil's Elbow of the epic duel between Giacomo Agostini on the MV-3, and John Cooper on the BSA-3, in the 1971 Race of the Year at Mallory Park. Above: crowds urge Cooper on through the 90 mph bend. Opposite: Ago's turn to lead.

Starting on January 28 1965, some road running was done with this engine, sufficient to establish the fact that a 'three' could operate more smoothly than a twin, using the same mountings. Also, we realised that the weight penalty was not too ridiculous. Generally, though, the engine ran too hot. By this time it was mid-1965 and the company was considering a new approach to the design of its road machines. The intention was to have a 250 single, a 500 twin, and a 750 'three', all with identical bore and stroke dimensions of 67 × 70 mm. Work was started on the 250, which went into production as a BSA. The 500 Triumph was redesigned with the new internal dimensions, but around that time the late Harry Sturgeon, managing director of the BSA-Triumph motorcycle division, decided that we must enter the model in the 1966 Daytona 200 classic. American competition rules insisted that a factory must produce 200 units of an engine before it was raced, but it was realised that this would not be possible with the new 500 engine in the time available. So the 500 was left with its original bore and stroke of 69 × 65.5 mm.

But with so much knowledge already gained on the 750 'threes', it was reasonable to incorporate the 67 × 70 mm bore and stroke into this design, and also to introduce many more worth-while changes. Head temperatures were reduced by raising the rocker box floor above the head joint. Cylinder head distortion at the joint with the barrel was cured by the use of an aluminium barrel. To save weight, we used dural instead of steel for the con rods, and based their dimensions on lessons learned with the 500 cc Daytona racers. The engine was unable to run continuously on the ordinary white metal Babbit bearings on the big end and in the mains, but Vandervell supplied the answer, in the form of a material used in certain high performance cars. Special twin ring scraper rings were fitted to the pistons, to cope with the engine's large oil supply.

The engine's potential crank speed demanded the use of high load type valve springs, so it was not surprising that cam wear became a problem. Chances could not be taken with a machine that was to go into production, and although the tappets were provided with an oil feed to the cams, the decision was taken to fit nitrided camshafts until such times as

one or the other of these items could be dispensed with. In fact, the nitrided cams have proved so good that recently the tappet-to-cam oiling scheme has been discontinued.

All the development findings were ploughed into the production models by Brian Jones' design team, and the three-cylinder machines, in the form of the Triumph Trident and the BSA Rocket-3, were announced in March 1968. They were greeted with tremendous enthusiasm world-wide, which was hardly surprising, for the idea of a three-cylinder 750 cc roadster was something of a sensation at that time, and the bikes were among the pioneers of the so-called 'superbike' era. They appeared several months before Honda got their 750 cc 'fours' on the market.

At first we had no thoughts of racing the new machines, because we were still being successful with our 500 cc Daytona racers, and with the 650 cc Bonneville twin in production racing. In fact no one really took 750 cc racing seriously at that time, partly because 500s were still lapping as fast as the bigger machines.

Percy Tait can claim the honour of actually racing a factory-entered 'three' for the first time, when he rode one in the production event in the Hutchinson 100 in 1969. He finished sixth, but we were not worried, as we had run the bike primarily to find out how it handled. It was good, although not very fast, since it was fitted with a standard engine. Prior to that, Ray Pickrell had ridden the bike in a private test session at Thruxton, where he crashed after lapping very quickly. Under pressure of our other racing operations, development of the 'three' was then suspended for the summer months.

In the autumn of 1969 we began to think seriously about racing the 'three', because our 650s were being pressed in the production class, and the open 750 cc class was growing in status. We fitted an engine with proven components similar to those on the 500 cc racer, and put it on the test bench. It immediately gave over 78 bhp, not necessarily with reliability, but the potential was there. Suspect parts included the valve seats, which were made of a rather soft material for the high loads involved, and the ignition system, which would not always give accurate timing at high rpm.

Meanwhile, Triumph had received a letter that was to have great significance. It came from the weekly newspaper *Motor Cycle News*, and it asked our views on the merits of production racing as opposed to F750 racing, as the paper was thinking of creating a new road racing series on British circuits. It was in answer to this circular that I first came out in favour of F750, or Daytona, type racing. In a memorandum to the company management, dated September 10 1969, I suggested that we should opt for an F750 type class. I wrote: 'The existing production racing scheme has gradually restricted development. Instead of using in production something that has been proved in racing, the rules ensure that no changes can be made, other than secret internal modifications of minor nature. Class 2 (F750) would eventually provide a competition department which would create a vast store of information on new approaches to problems, as a guide to our designers'.

By this time, the Americans had changed the rules of their events, making them open to all 750 cc machines. Up to 1969 they had limited ohv engines to 500 cc, but had allowed side-valve machines to run up to 750 cc. The company realised that, since we had an ohv 750 cc 'three' performing well on the test bed, we might be competitive at Daytona in 1970. In December 1969 the decision was taken—we would contest the American classic. Suddenly, we were going racing with the 'threes'.

We were not exactly strangers to success at Daytona, since we had won there in 1966 and 1967 with our 500 cc machines. But nevertheless, the decision to send six bikes to the 1970 event involved a massive effort. The three-cylinder road machines used four-speed gearboxes, but Rod Quaife, the gearbox specialist, supplied his special five-speed clusters for the racers. Rob North, the frame expert from Nuneaton, Warwickshire, designed a frame based on a chassis he had built for Percy Tait's 650 twin a year before. Graham Nicholson and Trevor Winship, two of our research workers who had experience of wind tunnel testing, helped in the design of fairings, which we tried on the bike at Elvington airfield in Yorkshire in January 1970, two months before the race was due to take place. The runway was covered in frost, but the sun was kind enough to come out for an hour and make it possible for Percy Tait to run the machine. He recorded a best speed of 164 mph, with a two-way average of 157 mph—very satisfying. Then the sun retired and Percy had to abandon the tests.

Before we left for America, the Daytona bikes were shown to the press, who were duly impressed. But I still think that the world in general did not take the venture very seriously, perhaps because they were not expecting us to go as fast as we did at Daytona. Perhaps, too, they were unused to the idea of a British factory fielding such a sophisticated design in a major international event.

But once we arrived in Daytona, the bikes became almost an overnight sensation. The 750 cc Harley-Davidsons, winners of the event for the past two years, were expected to dominate the race again. But in qualifying round the 2.5-mile banked speed bowl, we had the fastest three machines. Gene Romero averaged 157.34 mph on his Triumph, and went through a speed trap on the front straight at an incredible 165.44 mph. On his BSA, Mike Hailwood was second fastest round the bowl at 152.9 mph, and Gary Nixon took his Triumph round third fastest at 152.82 mph. In comparison, Cal Rayborn, Harley's best rider, could only manage 21st place in qualifying, at 145 mph.

The booming exhaust note of the 'threes', which was to become a trademark of their presence at race tracks in future years, made them stand out from all the other works machines. But in the team, we were far from happy. The fairings were aerodynamically excellent, but they tended to direct hot air from the engine on to the carburettors, causing a misfire. We had also experienced continual and unpredictable piston burning during practice week.

As it happened, this latter problem cost us the race. Hailwood led for 12 laps until he retired with pre-ignition. Later in the race, Nixon was leading, but he retired on the 32nd of the 53 laps—with a burnt piston. Percy Tait, who had taken a seventh machine to the race, retired with carburettor overheating, and Jim Rice stopped with a holed piston.

Dick Mann won the race on his 750 cc Honda-4, but Romero and Don Castro gave us

Doug Hele gives a satisfied smile as John Cooper collects the £1,050 winner's cheque at the 1971 Race of the Year from Motor Circuit Developments director Chris Lowe (right). Behind Cooper's left shoulder is his mechanic, Steve Brown.

second and third places on their factory Triumphs. Dave Aldana finished 12th, on one of our BSAs, after crashing and losing time.

We returned to Britain disappointed at having lost, but full of enthusiasm for the way the bikes had performed, and determined to solve the problems. We learned that the piston burning was caused by the combination of a high compression ratio—12:1—and slightly inaccurate control of the ignition timing under very hot conditions. Under severe temperatures, the timing would wander by four to five degrees. The solution was to design a new contact breaker assembly, and to smooth the piston off to give an 11.4:1 compression ratio.

The Daytona type 'threes' were not subjected to a real racing programme in Europe in 1970. Instead, we concentrated on the production version of the bike. Nortons won the 500-miler that year, while our works bike, ridden by Percy and Malcolm Uphill, retired with a broken valve stem tip while in third place. But we got our revenge, and our first big European win with the 'threes', in the Production TT in June. Paul Smart retired his Trident with a front wheel puncture when he was leading, but Malcolm beat Peter Williams, on the works Norton Commando, by just 1.6 seconds after 188 miles of racing. We also had the fastest five machines through the speed trap, with Bob Heath leading at 133.3 mph.

We scored an even greater success in the Bol d'Or 24-hour race in France later in the year. The works opposition from Honda, Norton, Laverda, Moto Guzzi and BMW was very strong, but Paul Smart and Tom Dickie rode the factory Trident to victory, covering 1,828 miles at an average speed of 76.51 mph, and breaking the race distance record by no less than 24 laps.

Meanwhile, we were still learning about the F750 racers. In outings at Thruxton and Castle Combe, Percy discovered that the frame which had proved so suitable on the slow infield turns at Daytona handled badly under the demands of British short circuit racing. We changed the head angle from 64 degrees to the 62 degrees used successfully on our racing 650 cc Bonnevilles, and that made all the difference. With the new frame, Paul finished fourth in the Hutchinson 100. Still more encouraging, he and Gary Nixon finished third and fourth in the Race of the Year at Mallory, behind winner John Cooper's 350 cc Yamsel. And Paul had had to climb through the field after failing to push-start his bike at the first attempt.

Soon after, the Daytona bike scored its first European win when we finished first, second and third in an F750 style event at the Brands Hatch Race of the South. But it was not a very satisfying victory, as the race was poorly supported.

At the end of the season we retired to our headquarters at Meriden to concentrate on extensive development before the 1971 Daytona race. At that time we had no idea of the tremendous successes in store for us in the following year. We knew we now had a reliable engine, but we wanted a little more power. Using our experience with the 500 cc racer once again, we adopted a squish piston which gave improved power and torque. In this form, the peak power increased to 84 bhp at the crankshaft at 8,500 rpm, and the engines were safe up to a 9,000 rpm limit.

Our new ignition system had already proved satisfactory, but we also had to relocate the oil cooler. In its normal position, just above the exhaust rocker boxes, it was still allowing hot air to circulate around the carburettors. We moved it to the nose of the fairing. The frame was modified to give a stiffer front end, the ground clearance was increased, and we replaced the 10-in diameter, four leading shoe Fontana front brake with twin discs. We

'So that is where they hide the turbocharger!' An MV mechanic examines a Triumph-3.

were already using a single disc at the rear. The dry weight of the machine was 370 lb, about the same as the previous year's machines.

We dominated that year's Daytona from start to finish. Our American team already had the six machines we had built for them in 1970, but we also gave them two completely new bikes, which Dick Mann and Gene Romero used. We also shipped over two development machines for Smart and Hailwood to ride. This meant that we had a total of ten works machines on the track, and all through practice week the circuit never really seemed free of the boom of one or other of the 'threes' streaming round the bankings.

Qualifying had been moved from the speed bowl to the actual 3.81-mile circuit which was used for the race. Of the 117 starters, Paul qualified fastest at 105.8 mph, although Cal Rayborn was a close second on the Harley, at 105.678 mph. During practice, the Champion Spark Plug man had warned us that we were running close to the limit with the very high 12.7:1 compression ratio on Paul's machine. But the engine gave no trouble prior to the race, so we decided not to change it.

When the race started, a then almost unknown rider named Gary Fisher disputed the lead with Mike and Paul until his 750 Honda retired. Then Mike stopped shortly afterwards with pushrod failure—a problem we had suspected might crop up. Later in the season we had to fit steel ends to the pushrods.

Paul took over the lead, and it gave me great satisfaction to see this fine rider, for whom I have so much respect, heading all the other bikes in a race which carries so much prestige in the vital American market. But his development bike also stopped, with a holed piston, when he had built up a 26-second lead with only a few laps remaining. We still scored a 1-2-3 victory, however, with Dick Mann and Don Emde taking their BSAs to first and third places, and Gene Romero finishing second on his Triumph. A privately entered Trident rider finished seventh, and Tom Rockwood was eighth on another of the works bikes. I was really pleased. Of the four new machines we had taken over, one had set the fastest qualifying time, two had led the race before retiring, and the remaining two had finished first and second. Rayborn's Harley had broken its gearbox on the first lap.

We returned from Daytona to be faced with the hectic demands of the Anglo-American match race series, which was being promoted for the first time. The company was heavily involved, as our American factory team brought over their 'threes' and pitted them against the British Triumph and BSA riders. The Britons won, in the three rounds held over four days at Easter, and the 60,000 spectators who watched the series enjoyed some spectacular racing.

After the match races, we turned to the major events of the European season. I would have preferred to run a simple two-man team, since this arrangement would have been easy to operate, providing good development knowledge from only a small labour force. But company policy was to give bikes to four riders on a regular basis—Paul Smart, Ray Pickrell, Tony Jefferies and Percy Tait, the factory development rider. Bob Heath also received occasional rides.

You may say that each of the riders gave us excellent results. This is true, but you must draw the line somewhere. As it was, the mechanics were logging 60 hours a week, without counting the time they spent at race meetings at weekends. We had to maintain five F750 bikes and three production machines.

The team dominated British short-circuit events, and finished first and second in both the 500-mile production race at Thruxton, and in the 200-mile F750 event, which was incorporated into the main race. An F750 race was included in the TT programme for the first time in 1971, and I was expecting the bikes to give handling problems. But on the 37¾-mile Mountain circuit we found that the strong frames and the excellent steering geometry made them handle well. Tony Jefferies won the race at an average of 102.85 mph, setting the fastest lap at 103.21 mph. Ray finished second, ahead of Peter Williams' Norton, to give us a 1-2. Then Ray won the Production race on a Trident, setting the first

ever over-100 mph average for the race, at 100.07 mph. Tony and Bob Heath finished second and third.

Early in September, we repeated our 1970 victory in the most important motorcycle race in France, the Bol d'Or 24-hour marathon. Again, there was considerable works opposition, but our rival teams seemed to base their motorcycles on our winning standard of the year before. But we arrived with a much faster machine which used a 1970 Daytona frame and an engine built to full Daytona specifications. Ray and Percy rode it to victory, beating a factory Laverda by seven laps.

On occasions during the summer, John Cooper had asked me about the possibility of getting further rides on the BSA-3 he had used in the match races. I had always turned down his suggestion, not because I had any bias against John, but because of the pressure we faced in maintaining machinery for the existing team. But the company had promised John a bike for the Race of the Year at Mallory Park in September, and this had to be adhered to. So John came back into the team, an event that marked the beginning of the most remarkable month in the story of the 'threes'.

Our chief opposition at Mallory was to be the Italian multiple world champion, Giacomo Agostini, and his 500 cc three-cylinder MV grand prix machine. Agostini was considered to be almost unbeatable on the MV, and although there was some speculation about whether our roadster-based 750s could stop him, I did not really consider this to be possible.

Early in the year, it was true, Paul had given Agostini a shock in two races in South Africa, when he had forced him to break the lap record on each occasion, and had finished only 6.5 and 5.5 seconds behind. We had been pushing the MV, and this was great, but we still didn't know how far we had extended Ago.

I thought that if anyone was going to beat Agostini at Mallory, it could only be Paul. I never considered John as a potential winner. It was his first race on the bike since Easter, and his engine was not giving as much power as some of our other machines. He also fell off his 250 cc Yamaha during practice.

My hopes received a blow when Paul's engine, a much used unit, blew up in one of the

'Threes' on the TT course. Left: Tony Jefferies, winner of the first F750 race in 1971, swings through Ramsey. Right: Ray Pickrell, double TT winner on Triumph-3s in 1972, at Ballaugh Bridge.

races preceding the Race of the Year. He took over the Trident we had loaned to Gary Nixon, but it meant he would be using an unfamiliar machine.

I watched the race from the finish area, and it turned into the most breathtaking and exciting event I have ever seen. I got my first shock when John came through on the opening lap leading Agostini. However, I never attach too much importance to placings on the first lap, because faster riders may have been baulked at the start.

John came round with Ago for a second time, and then I thought I was seeing the impossible when he continued to stay with him as the race drew on. It seemed that John must surely drop back when he had a big slide at the Esses at half distance, and Ago got by on the next lap. But the MV didn't pull away, and instead John repassed at the Esses on the 22nd of the 30 laps. It was at this point that I first realised we could win. John had gone through a nasty moment, but had still been able to recover and get back into the lead. He was never passed again, and he took the flag 0.6 seconds ahead of the MV.

I think this race must be rated as the greatest of all the victories we scored with the 'threes'. On our roadster-based racer we had beaten the world champion and the fastest grand prix machine in racing. I suddenly realised that I hadn't appreciated before Mallory what a remarkable rider John Cooper is.

The following week, at the Cadwell international, Ago was beaten again, this time by Derek Chatterton and his 350 cc Chat Yamaha. John finished third, and already some people were saying that his Mallory performance had been a fluke. But seven days later, at the Brands Hatch Race of the South, John and the BSA beat Agostini for a second time, and on this occasion in an even more decisive fashion. He passed the MV on the second lap, was never headed again, and broke the absolute lap record for the 2.65-mile circuit, leaving it at 91.03 mph.

Our next major event was the inaugural 250-mile Champion Spark Plug Classic, which was to be run over two 125-mile heats on the 3.2-mile circuit inside the vast Ontario Motor Speedway in California. We flew over a Triumph Trident for Gary Nixon, and the Ago-beating BSA for John. The company's American organisation had also entered their three-cylinder machines.

Gary won the first leg from Yvon Du Hamel, on the 500 cc works Kawasaki, with John, who had been baulked at the start, in third place, ahead of Kel Carruthers' 350 cc Yamaha. When Gary got away in first place in the second leg, it seemed he must win the event overall. But on the second lap he hit a patch of oil and slid off on a fast corner. John was right behind him, but on a slightly wider line, and he missed the oil, as did Kel. But Du Hamel, Dick Mann, Cliff Carr, Ron Grant and Dave Aldana all went down on the oil.

It meant that either John or Kel must win the race, and they battled on through the remaining miles. In the confusion of Gary's crash I had lost count of the number of laps that had passed, and both John and I were caught out when the white flag to signal the last lap suddenly went out, when Kel was holding the lead.

I watched for them to come out of the final turn on the last lap. People who saw the race disagree with me over the distance between the two at that point, but I say that as they came on to the finishing straight the gap between Kel in the lead and John in second place was at least 200 yards.

I thought then that the race was over, that we had lost, and I was feeling thoroughly fed up because I blamed myself for not keeping track of the race and warning John of how many laps were left. I began picking up tyres and tools in our pit, without even watching the bikes come up the straight. But as I looked up again they flashed across the finish line and it almost looked as if John had won. But I decided it was too silly to be true, and dismissed the thought. Then the commentator was saying that John had done it, and I realised that Coop had won this race in an even more surprising manner than he had beaten Ago.

It was from this race that I learnt how easy Cooper is on any machine he rides. He races them almost as if he has paid for every nut and bolt. At Ontario, his rev counter was run-

Percy Tait, the first man ever to race a factory-entered Triumph-3, takes a production Trident round Brands Hatch.

ning slightly fast, and until the last lap I don't think he had run the engine at over 8,000 rpm. On that final desperate run home, when he had to wind on everything, the rev counter needle showed 10,000 rpm, although 9,500 was a truer figure.

Ontario was the final race of the season, and when we got back to England the factory gave considerable thought to our racing activities. We had won the two most publicised events of the year—Daytona and Ontario—we had beaten the MV, we had won the new *Motor Cycle News* Superbike Championship, the TT, the Bol d'Or, the 500-miler, and the 750 cc British championship. But we also knew that the racing was preventing my department from developing new road machines, an even more vital project for the future.

So we made the decision to cut back on our racing, and supply John Cooper, Ray Pickrell and Tony Jefferies with machines on a semi-works basis. No development was put into the bikes during the winter of 1971-72, yet during the 1972 season they were still fast enough to win the major events in Britain. On his Trident, Ray Pickrell won three rounds of the Easter match race series, with Harley's Cal Rayborn taking the other three rounds. Ray also won both the Production and the Formula 750 TTs, setting a new lap record in the latter race at 105.68 mph. If he had been pressed, I'm sure he could have lapped at over 106 mph. Ray also looked like winning the Superbike Championship, until he suffered that very severe accident at Mallory late in the season, when he fractured his pelvis. John Cooper eventually won the Championship, with Ray in second place.

At the close of the 1972 season we announced our decision to withdraw completely from racing in Britain, in order to give the design and development staff the chance to put maximum effort into our road machines. Predictably, the decision was not popular with many people, because we had provided so much excitement and entertainment on the racing circuits for the past three years. But really there is nothing odd about a motorcycle factory dismantling its racing team. Honda have done it twice, once from GP competition, and again after they won at Daytona in 1970. I feel sure that if we had developed the machines further for the 1973 season, we could have continued to win major international events. We would have designed a new cylinder head, pared perhaps 30 lb from the weight, and fitted a new fairing and certain new internal engine parts.

But there were other considerations. The foreign opposition in the market place had become so great that the design, development and production of our road models demanded the efforts of everyone connected with the factory. Some sacrifice had to be made, and the immediate area to suffer was the racing programme. We all know the advantage in publicity that racing has given us. But there comes a time when the motorcycle going down the production line must be the prime consideration. Anyone who insists that we should have carried on racing, a) doesn't realise the effort it had taken to get us where we were in 1971 and '72, and b) doesn't appreciate the percentage of top engineering staff that a massive racing programme absorbs.

The team that made all our racing successes possible includes, of course, the mechanics: Steve Brown, Bill Fannon, Arthur Jakeman, Fred Swift, Jack Shemans and John Woodward. Les Williams, himself a top class fitter, was in charge of the racing shop, and Norman Hyde, one of my engineering assistants, gave constant help. We also had the support of the design staff, the toolroom and Alan Barrett's experimental department. Bert Hopwood, who is now a member of the group's parent board and the director of engineering, has always given me the scope and guidance to go racing, and the former engineering director of the motorcycle division, Mike Nedham, offered considerable moral support.

When this fine team was switched from racing activities, it did not mean that their talents were lost. Instead, they began work once again on improving the British motorcycle product that reaches the customer. Selling machines, after all, is a motorcycle factory's prime consideration. And by doing so, the result, hopefully, will be that we shall be able to return to racing in the future.

CHAPTER 7

On three wheels

by John Brown, road racing reporter, 'Motor Cycle News'

MAKE NO MISTAKE about it, sidecar racers are a world apart from their more glamorised solo riding counterparts. They contest events on the same programme as solo riders, but any similarity between the two classes ends there.

Even the personal make-up and attitude to the sport of a sidecar driver or passenger bears absolutely no similarity to that of the two-wheel racer. Perhaps the reason is that the sidecar class has always been a 'Cinderella' affair, receiving less prize and start money—at meetings where there is such a luxury as the latter—and a lot less publicity. To a large degree the press can be blamed for the lack of headlines, in the way they frequently tuck the sidecar race at the end of a report on a meeting, even if it has been the closest event of the day.

Because of this general attitude towards them, the sidecar brigade tend to keep themselves to themselves, although I think it would be unfair to suggest that they bear any real grudge about their position. Of course, there does come the united cry of 'Give us a fair crack of the whip,' when they feel the sidecar race deserves a little more prominence.

The 'us' part of the plea rather underlines the characteristic closeness of sidecar competitors. They speak as a united body, in sharp contrast to the more individual approach of solo riders even now after the successful formation of the Grand Prix Riders Association, which is dominated by the solo men. The very united feeling among the chair boys must be one of the main reasons that this section of the sport continues to flourish, despite the sidecar outfit's almost complete disappearance from use on the public roads.

Britain, too, remains the stronghold of sidecar racing, although the West Germans have dominated the world championships, supplying both riders and machines for the last 20 years. The last time Britain had a sidecar world champion was back in 1953 when Eric Oliver took the title with a Norton-powered outfit, an achievement, incidentally, that marked the last world championship success for a British machine in any road racing class. But although the West Germans always keep the best BMW outfits for themselves to ensure world championship domination, Britain must still have more sidecar competitors than any other country. Currently some 150 crews regularly contest events at international, national and club meetings throughout the country every weekend during the eight-month season.

The ability differs dramatically, but at the top there are drivers capable of beating the best from Germany, if only they had competitive machinery. Unfortunately, the best a British driver can hope for is a well prepared engine originally intended for road use, which can hardly be expected to match the power of the special racing units used by the Germans. The brightest British hope since the Oliver era is Chris Vincent, the Birmingham-born sidecar driver who now pilots a world-beating Munch four-cylinder outfit. This engine, designed especially for racing—by a German, of course—has proved capable of breaking the BMW domination on two occasions, once in the hands of its original creator, Helmut Fath, and again in 1971 when West German Horst Owesle emerged as world champion at his first attempt.

Extensive modifications to convert the sidecar from the right hand side of the machine, a location favoured by the Continentals, to the left to suit the British style took longer than anticipated, and consequently Vincent was hardly ready for the early championship rounds in 1972. But Vincent, seven times a British champion, proved his world class ability by beating the 1972 champion Klaus Enders in the Finnish GP, the final round of the season.

So Vincent is the lucky one, while most British sidecar drivers soldier on, knowing that their chances of reaching the pinnacle of success are almost non-existent. Perhaps this is one of the main reasons why British short circuit racing attracts so much attention from the chair men, and why the racing is so competitive. A sidecar outfit is a far more personal thing than any solo motorcycle, for it is impossible to buy a complete over-the-counter three-wheeler. True, a small number of firms specialise in the manufacture of racing outfits, but they only produce to order and, in most circumstances, do not provide the engine and gearbox. So most crews build their own outfits, and for many this is as much of a challenge as the actual racing.

Although a sidecar crew work on their outfit in their own time, and to their own design,

Variety on the front row at Silverstone: George O'Dell (750 BSA twin, 14), Rudi Kurth (500 Monark-3 water-cooled two-stroke, 3), Gerry Boret (500 Konig-4 water-cooled two-stroke, 50), Chris Vincent (750 Munch-4, 2), and world champion Klaus Enders (500 BMW flat twin, 1).

they certainly do not get their racing on the cheap. Far from it, for in hard cash, materials and fittings will put a price tag of around £400 on an outfit. And that sum does not consider construction time that can literally run into hundreds of hours. Roy Hanks, the youngest of the famous sidecar racing family from Birmingham, recently spent six months working on a new outfit, and he was helped by two other skilled workmen. 'The cost of building a good machine is almost crippling,' he comments. 'People just don't realise the expense involved, and that is why we are made the poor relation on so many occasions by race organisers.'

The first major decision the sidecar constructor must face is what type of engine he should use and, though this may sound odd, where he is to find it. For he cannot begin to build or even plan the machine without first making a choice of power unit, for the layout and outer dimensions of the engine will determine so many other features of the outfit. While the 650 cc BSA and Triumph twin-cylinder units remain the most popular engines among sidecar drivers, they cannot be bought brand new as separate components from the factories or from dealers. Factory policy is to supply only complete motorcycles. So the desperate sidecar builder must either seek out an engine from a crashed machine, or go to the cost of buying a new road-going bike. In the latter case, he can hope to reclaim a few pounds by selling the cycle parts.

Once the power unit has been obtained, basic tuning has to be carried out. Costs here can be minimised if the builder can do much of the work himself, but riders with less mechanical ability will extend the bill by enlisting the help of experienced engine tuners.

The basic power requirement needed from a BSA A65 or Triumph Bonneville engine is around 52 bhp. This is quite sufficient for club racing or early attempts at national status events. Then comes the need for more power. Leading British circuit riders like Roy Hanks and his elder brother Norman reckon on getting about 70 bhp from BSA engines which can be enlarged to almost 750 cc after tuning and modification in the never ending quest for more speed. Chris Vincent went even further and reached the upper 70s with the BSA engine he used in 1971, but this level of development costs money and demands real expertise in engine work. Power outputs this great also require considerable riding skill and experience before they can be used to advantage.

Some engineering companies now offer conversion kits which bring the BSA and Triumph motors up to a full 750 cc. But the Hanks brothers, with the help of father Fred, who acts as a test driver by using the latest experimental engines in his occasional outings, now have their own 742 cc and 820 cc versions of the original BSA 654 cc unit. Roy's 742 cc engine has a 79 mm stroke, four mm longer than standard, but it retains the original 75 mm bore. The bigger engine has been stroked up to 80 mm and is almost 'square', with a 79 mm bore.

Says Roy: 'Our first attempt to increase the engine capacity was restricted to lengthening the stroke. The first problem we encountered was crankshaft seizure because the crank was oil fed from the end and this method was not sufficient for the extra power. The crank ran on a bush and this either seized or started rattling after every meeting. It meant a change after each race, and to overcome this we substituted roller bearings. To get the size up to 820 cc for Norman's engine we went a step further and added special oversize barrels. This was successful but our recent move to increase an engine to 848 cc has not been too hopeful. It has run into all sorts of troubles that we have never encountered before.'

For less demanding riders, basic modifications to an engine to make it a competitive sidecar racing unit involve almost all the internal parts. Work on the exhaust and inlet ports, the valves and the crankshaft is of prime importance. A complete strip-down, methodic preparation of all the parts and the careful reassembly of the engine often suffices with a new motor, although some parts will usually have to be replaced in a second-hand engine. When extra power is sought special engine components have to be

No wonder sidecar racing is popular with the crowds! Going into Druids Bend during a 'wrong way round' Hutchinson 100 at Brands, Norman Hanks leads brother Roy. Coming out, Roy has reversed the positions, as Norman applies opposite lock to the BSA.

fitted and the value of the engine can more than double. Special bearings can cost as much as £60 for a BSA engine, while racing cams will be even more. The outlay is endless and just one engine blow-up can set its owner back well over £100.

Tony Wakefield and Graham Milton, two drivers from Huntingdonshire, are persevering with their own development of the BMW engine. They have already been successful with the 500 cc long-stroke Rennsport unit. Now they are working on extensively modified versions of the 750 cc R75 BMW flat twin engine. Absolutely every part of the motor has been modified and almost everything has been made as one-off parts in their private race workshop. So far they have been unable to work out the cost—true figures are always impossible to obtain in projects like this—but it runs into hundreds of pounds. They have raised the power output from the standard 57 bhp at 6,400 rpm to over 70 bhp at 7,500 rpm. It is a successful exercise, and one that underlines the mechanical skill that is more prominent among sidecar drivers than in solo riders.

Most drivers have very personal views on chassis design for a racing outfit. A few buy this component from one of the firms who offer a ready made chassis kit, but most crews make their frames in their own workshops. It's quite amazing how much chassis development has taken place over the years. When Oliver last won the world title for Britain, outfits were basically normal solo racing machines with a sidecar bolted on. Today, the framework of the entire machine is constructed as a single unit, and the conventional sitting-up style of riding a motorcycle has been replaced by the 'kneeler' position that was introduced to British circuits for the first time by Ted Young in the late 'fifties. It was a fashion that really caught on, and over the years has led to the sophistication in sidecar design that can be seen on the circuits today.

The advancement is incredible, but it does indicate once again that the majority of sidecar racers see the challenge of competition start in the workshop. Sidecar racing is a better outlet than solo racing for the mechanically minded rider, and while it offers this sort of attraction the class will remain strong.

'King of drift' Chris Vincent and passenger Mike Casey at work on the mighty Munch four-cylinder outfit. Vincent made his return to world championship racing on this machine in 1972 and won the Finnish GP.

Works support is rare in sidecar racing, so riders have to maintain their own machinery. Here, Peter Hanks (left), a non-racing member of the famous sidecar family, assists brother Roy.

The tubing used to make a chassis will cost about £30. The most popular type is the seam-free Reynolds 531, and for an average outfit some five different sizes will be used. Most of the frame will be constructed of 1¼ inch diameter tubing, and about ten yards of this will be required, plus about five yards of 1 inch diameter material.

Cast alloy wheels cost about £30 each, and tyres £10 each. A conventional 16 inch motorcycle rear tyre will last for only about three 15-lap races, depending on the circuit. Twisty Cadwell Park is hard on tyres, Snetterton, with its fast straights, is kinder, and Brands Hatch and Oulton come in between the two. Many drivers now favour the 10 or 12 inch diameter wheels designed for mini saloon car racing. These allow wider tyres to be used, and they do extend rear tyre life by perhaps an extra race. A sidecar tyre has almost double the life of a rear wheel tyre, and the front tyre comes in between.

Glass fibre work adds about £80 to the cost of building an outfit, and the braking system will take another £30. Even a minor item such as a properly upholstered sidecar floor, essential if the outfit is going to look smart and provide safety and comfort for the passenger, can add another £3. A realistic value to place on an outfit used by one of the country's top crews would be around £750.

The financial outlay continues when the outfit is wheeled out of the workshop. Yet a passenger has to be considered where prize money is concerned. As an example, at a recent Silverstone international meeting, a first prize of £80 was offered for each of two 15-lap sidecar races. But solo riders racing over the same distance were offered £100 for being first over the line. As Vincent puts it: 'I see no reason why we should be £20 down on the solos. Even if we got the same prizes we would be worse off because we have a passenger to share the money with'.

It is simply proof that the sidecar men are battling against a 'second class citizen' tag.

Scenes like this were frequent in the 'sixties when Owen Greenwood challenged the conventional sidecars with his controversial Greenwood Mini cyclecar. Here, Greenwood (24) is surrounded by the BSA-powered outfits of Norman Hanks (10), Chris Vincent (6) and, at the rear, Peter Brown.

Entry fees for meetings are about the same as for solos, and when insurance is included average about £3.50 a race. Transport is an expensive item, with £5 as an average petrol bill per meeting. Depreciation on the transporter absorbs a further £5 a week, and with tax and insurance to consider a racer can reckon on a total outlay, including fuel, of £15 a week if he runs one of the popular Thames or Transit vans. This figure does not include maintenance, which many crews perform themselves to save money that can be better spent on the outfit.

The outfit itself should be able to complete four or five meetings of the Mallory Park and Brands Hatch standard before a complete engine strip-down is required. But expenses will soar if the crew contest the TT. Roy Hanks had to spend almost £150 on reconditioning his engine after he raced in the Isle of Man in 1972.

Race clothing is another outlay to be considered, with leathers and a modern helmet costing about £30 each. Sidecar racers have a unique problem with boots. On kneeler outfits, the driver's right boot tends to scrape the track surface as he leans out on right-hand bends. In this way a boot can become a tattered remnant in three meetings. The Hanks brothers eventually became so annoyed at having to throw away perfectly usable left boots that they persuaded a manufacturer to make an extra batch of right foot boots. Sidecar ingenuity won again!

On the track, racing an outfit is essentially a team effort, and it is this complete contrast to the solo events that gives sidecar racing so much of its spectator appeal. The crowds enjoy it because they see a real spectacle when two people are working together to get a machine round a circuit as quickly as possible. To them it does not matter that it is impossible to associate anything about a racing sidecar with any type of machine they see on the public roads.

Some circuits are more suited to sidecar racing than others, and none more so than the 1.35-mile Mallory Park venue, which Norman Hanks describes as 'hectic'.

'The corners come up so quickly on such a small lap that there is little time to really think much about it', he says. 'There is no time to communicate with the passenger. He has to be left to his own devices far more than on possibly any other circuit. There's no knocking him on the shoulder as a signal to get over the back wheel or lean out a little further. You have to leave everything to him and hope he does the right thing at the right time. It's a question of getting a smooth rhythm while racing and, on the passenger's part, reaching a complete understanding of what the driver is going to do. A passenger can make or break you at Mallory. If he gets over-enthusiastic and puts his weight over the back wheel too quickly or too soon he can kill the engine dead. Once the speed and ground are lost it is almost impossible to catch up.'

Mallory is also a busy circuit for the driver and for the four-speed 740 cc twin-cylinder outfit that Hanks drives it is almost a flat-out-in-third operation. He explains: 'From a push start, with the engine engaged in first gear, it's a flat-out acceleration test along the 200-yard straight to Gerards bend. This long right-handed sweep should be taken in third without shutting off so that it's possible to drop momentarily into top gear for the Stebbe Straight, the fastest section on the circuit. I don't take the revs over 6,000 so I should reach somewhere between 100 and 105 mph approaching the right and left swerve through the Esses. It's back down to third, but no more, and I drive hard through the section. It is possible to take the Esses in fourth gear but you lose the drive for the exit, although some crews seem to prefer to stay in top and rush into the corner faster.

'From the Esses it's a quick sprint up to the hairpin, hard on in third, before knocking it down to second for the final approach. There's a lot of sorting out here, especially on the first lap, and there is a temptation to use the engine as a brake. But the best way is to ease the speed with the brakes, and then change down to first gear for the corner itself. Once round it's back into second as quickly as possible, to counteract the wheelspin that so easily develops with the machine in bottom gear. The few yards to the top of Devils Elbow is not long enough to allow for relaxation. It's back into third, peel off to the left, and drive flat-out down the dip holding the bars with a grip like steel. Again it's possible to drop into top for a short distance before we reach Gerards again, but from then on a

This is how sidecar racing used to look. Compare this scene at the Mallory Park Vintage Race of the Year meeting with the preceding shots of the Hanks brothers' machinery.

flying lap is tackled in a similar way to the first one. Depending on gearing it is possible to round Gerards flat out in top, but I prefer to keep in third. The most essential part on this corner is not to lose the drive. If you do, it can mean a 20-yard gain for the opposition. Gerards is not my personal strong point and I am still experimenting to see if I can improve my speed round there. One of the reasons is that I am using big 16-inch wheels on my outfit and I seem to be getting worse round the bend as lap speeds increase. I intend to try 12-inch wheels as these are said to give far better traction. On a flying lap it may be possible to get down Stebbe Straight a little quicker, but I would say my maximum is about 105 mph, and there are few outfits quicker down there. Once the pressure is off I drop into top gear between the Esses and the hairpin, but this is more to give the engine a rest than anything else. As I have stressed, engine life can be extended by not using the motor as a brake for the fast approaches to corners, but in a close scrap it's not always so easy to remember that, and the chance to make up a little distance by leaving everything to the last minute is a temptation. And I can only stress that the work of the passenger is vital. He must not be too eager to get over the back wheel for right-handers, and on the left-handers he must hang out of the chair as low as possible to cut down wind resistance. For me, Mallory means team work at its best.'

When all the problems facing a sidecar driver are considered, such as not being able to buy a brand-new ready-to-race machine, and competing for minimal financial rewards, it's remarkable that anyone really bothers. Just what makes these people go sidecar racing instead of settling for the less complex life of a solo rider? It's a question that even the riders seem unsure about.

Until 25 years ago the bulk of sidecar drivers were ex-solo riders who became too old for two wheels and switched to the relative safety of three. Bill Boddice, Bill Beevers and Fred Hanks are but three well known examples. Pre-war and early post-war racing saw an average age of between 35 and 40 for sidecar drivers, and most of them were family men. The racing outfit was then a direct descendant of the road-going motorcycle combination, which was not only a favourite means of family travel, but also one that was considered to

Women passengers have always been a frequent sight in sidecar racing. This is Dane Rowe, passenger to Swiss driver Rudi Kurth.

Sidecar racing gives engineers maximum scope in machine construction. This 20-year-old 1,000 cc Vincent engine has been built into a modern 'kneeler' chassis, with leading link front suspension and twin disc front brakes.

be the safest, by the enthusiasts themselves, as well as by the insurance companies. Since the outfit was such a popular means of road transport, it was hardly surprising that a racing class for such machines grew up rapidly. Now, all that has completely changed. Riders start younger, often while still in their teens, and today only a few sidecar drivers have made the switch from solo racing. The machinery has developed to the stage where it bears no resemblance to road-going vehicles, and the challenge is taken up to race something completely unique. In a word, sidecars have now become a 'freak' class of racing.

Vincent is one of the few drivers currently in action who has also been a top solo racer. He finally settled for sidecars when he found himself in the lucky and rare position of being able to buy parts at a reasonable price, which made it cheaper for him to race sidecars than solos. His background made him a natural solo racer, however, for he was employed as a test rider for BSA and Norton. True, he had had his sidecar interest stimulated while he worked at the Norton factory in Birmingham, because at that time Oliver and Cyril Smith were receiving works support. But nobody considered young Vincent to be worth bothering with when it came to chair racing. When Associated Motor Cycles took over the Norton factory, Vincent returned to BSA and finally got the break that enabled him to enter sidecar racing.

'There were some parts available, so I had the chance to make a competitive outfit for much less than it was costing me to race solos,' says Vincent, who successfully combined both branches of the sport for almost five years before he switched completely to sidecars. He first won the British sidecar championship in 1961, and took the crown a further six times in the next ten years—quite a record.

No matter which driver you ask, the underlining factor that makes them go sidecar racing is the strong feeling of companionship that exists among them. 'It's great. I would never want to go solo racing again,' says Londoner George O'Dell, one of sidecar racing's youngsters, who has limited experience of solo racing.

For riders like the Hanks brothers and Mick Boddice, sidecar racing is really a matter

Rudi Kurth's GP outfit, powered by a 500 cc Crescent three-cylinder two-stroke engine, features monocoque chassis design.

of following in a famous father's footsteps. Fred Hanks, the father of the Hanks family, still manages a few races and, possibly more than anyone else in the sport, appreciates the different approach that now exists from his heyday. 'It used to be a real struggle in those days,' he recalls. 'I can remember borrowing the rent money and the coal money to go racing and then running out of cash before we got home. One day the van ran out of petrol 15 miles from home and we simply hadn't got a penny. So we had to leave the van for three days until we got paid and could afford more petrol.'

That really is racing on a shoestring, but it is an incident that shows the determination and enthusiasm of sidecar racers. For although all the material things have changed about the sport and there is a new young breed of driver, this type of spirit still exists. It is shown at any meeting at the Lydden circuit in Kent. The two consolation races there carry no prize money, not even for the winner, but the grids are always full and the efforts put in by the drivers are just as strong as among those battling for a first place in a big money international. They are simply racing for enjoyment.

Enthusiasm among drivers has never been higher, and the sport remains popular with the crowds. It has overcome the demise of the road-going motorcycle and sidecar, the end of support from British factories and, probably the most serious crisis that ever threatened its existence, the emergence of the tricar, or cyclecar.

Following a successful venture by Owen Greenwood in the mid-'sixties, when he produced a tricar powered by a Mini car engine, the purists feared that the traditional outfit was in real danger. The Greenwood machine bore more resemblance to a racing car than to a motorcycle, yet it met the legal design requirements for three-wheeler racing laid down by the ACU. It was also faster and far easier to drive than a conventional sidecar outfit. It did not even need a passenger as a balancing force on corners, for example, although the rules demanded that one had to be carried. Other machines followed in the Greenwood mould and cries of protest went up, although top drivers like Vincent worked to meet the challenge with their normal outfits. Eventually, the tricar was restricted to club and national events and then, from 1972, it was given a class of its own. But by then Greenwood had retired and support for the class had disappeared. Entries were not forthcoming and the 'freak' sidecar class had won another battle for existence. Now, it is as strong as ever and with a united backing, will be around for as long as road racing exists.

CHAPTER 8

A sponsor's story

by Vincent Davey, entrant, Gus Kuhn racing team

WHEN THE IDEA to become involved in racing as a sponsor occurred to me at the 1968 Barcelona 24-hour race, I had no idea that it would gradually evolve into a passion that today occupies as much of my time as running my motorcycle business. I had gone to Spain mainly on holiday, but also to watch the team entered by a friend, Stan Shenton, who was already involved in sponsorship at that time. I was hardly a racing fanatic in those days. I used to visit the TT every year, but I probably wouldn't even have gone there if I hadn't been able to play golf on the Island at the same time.

But once the idea of entering my own machines under the Gus Kuhn Motors banner came up, it became more appealing, for it coincided with a number of other happenings. At that time I had decided to drop the car side of the business and concentrate fully on motorcycles. The 750 cc Norton Commando had just been introduced as one of the very few new models to arrive on the scene in the late 'sixties. Some property adjoining our premises in London's Clapham Road had just been compulsorily purchased by the council, so this gave me some money to spend. And finally, I thought we could give Stan Shenton some competition and provide us both with a bit of fun. We still have this friendly rivalry going, and we quite often have side bets with each other, usually involving bottles of vino.

I got down to business right from the start. One quarter of our workshop was separated from the rest and devoted solely to racing preparation. It may be forgotten by many these days, when we see so many Norton Commandos on the race tracks, but we were the first to consider racing the Commando, and we had some early successes with it. But looking back on our early attempts, I realise that we wasted many days, even weeks, chasing up blind alleys trying this and that.

We tried to make a racer out of a standard Commando by retaining the original frame and shortening the forks and rear suspension units. We also made the bottom frame tubes narrower to take advantage of the machine's lower profile. But although we learnt a lot from this project, it never really worked. The bike did break the lap record at Lydden, ridden by Charlie Sanby, but I think Charlie liked the power and put up with the handling.

The problem was that the machine was not stable enough, and tried to leap about too much. Even the standard Commando occasionally shakes its head and our modifications only accentuated this tendency. With our present experience, however, I am confident we

Challenging the works bikes: Dave Potter (14) gets the Gus Kuhn Commando alongside Ray Pickrell's factory-entered Triumph Trident during the production race at the Hutchinson 100 in 1972.

CASTROL MOTORCYCLE RACING MANUAL

can make a competitive Formula 750 racer for the average rider by using the standard Commando frame and forks.

My first big success was when Mick Andrew won the 1969 Hutchinson 100, against works Triumphs and Nortons, and beating the BSA of Tony Smith by only six inches. Mick followed this by placing second to Agostini and beating Phil Read's 350 Yamaha at the Race of the South, something we did not think was possible. This was on a 750 engine that we had worked into a Mk II Seeley frame, without the blessing of Colin Seeley, who was not too keen at that time to give us something that would help us beat his 500s. He was quite happy afterwards, though, when we had success and his frame was given some credit for it. We have always used Seeley frames in our short circuit racers and have never regretted it. We now have so much experience with them that we would not change without a very good reason. Colin's frames allow you plenty of room to work on the bike and to fit components such as exhaust pipes. They make for fine handling bikes, and his swinging arm arrangement incorporating needle roller bearings is the best available.

From the start I decided to give all our machines the same handling and braking characteristics, to enable the riders to jump off one and on to another. This, in my view, is very important as a rider must be familiar with all the controls and procedures of a machine. This is one reason why we invariably get good starts. I never cease to be amazed at the number of top line riders who do not practice starts and repeatedly get off the grid way down the field. However, under the new rules on Motor Circuit Developments' tracks, with clutch starts being required, we have now lost our advantage on push starts, which was simply a question of practice and good preparation.

In my first years of sponsorship I spent between £4,000 and £5,000 annually on racing. I think I've now got it down to around £4,000 a year, as I have discovered how to control costs, and how to get some return into the kitty by means of start money, prize money and the odd contribution from other trade people. Generally speaking, my arrangement with riders is to divide prize and start money 50/50 but we pay all the costs of preparation, transportation and accommodation. It is difficult to keep costs down if you have ambitions. I have two mechanics working on nothing else but race bikes during the season, and in winter we generally build two new bikes. This does not include production racers, as we reckon to build them in one week when we have to.

Our current stock of raceware comprises one 24-hour bike, one production racer, three Formula 750 racers and another F750 model fitted with an 810 cc engine. We have three spare engines—one is a 500 cc unit—three spare gearboxes, plus a caravan and a van to transport it all.

Our engines are prepared by Jim Boughen. I reckon he must have more experience on the twin-cylinder Norton engine than anyone alive today. Certainly, if one considers how many engines on the race track he is responsible for, he must be way ahead of anyone else on volume alone.

Jim used to work in the race department at AMC's Plumstead factory on 7R and G50 racing engines. When Norton moved in from Birmingham he became responsible for the Norton twin-cylinder engines used on all the factory race machines, not that they had many. It's one of our jokes that he now works on more Norton racing engines for me than he ever did for Norton. He operates from his home and is a full-time tuner, working on nothing else but engines. He also happens to be a super cook and a connoisseur of food and wines, which makes him a doubly pleasant man to know! We work together very well and we do make progress. This is where we are very lucky in having several bikes with seven or eight engines in total. We have a good feedback of information and get immediate answers when we try different valve sizes, compression ratios and other modifications. People always imagine we use lots of exotic parts, but this is not the case. We use completely standard valve springs, cam followers and pushrods on our race motors. We also use mineral oils, the same as you can buy.

Our method of going racing is the tried and true one of finding out what works best and setting everything up spot-on. We now have several types of set-up for different circuits and 24-hour races, involving camshafts to be used with varying compression ratios, exhaust pipes and inlet manifold lengths. We know what sort of performance we get from different motors and can now approach the various circuits with more confidence. Don't think that, once you get a bike running well, you can cart it from circuit to circuit without altering anything except the gearing. Silverstone, for instance, demands a suspension set-up similar to the arrangement we have used at the TT. This may sound strange, since one is a converted airfield circuit and the other is a natural road course, but it illustrates the unlikely problems that crop up in racing. We went to Silverstone in 1972 with a bike that had been set up for Brands Hatch. But Dave Potter found that some of the fast bends at Silverstone have ripples that almost threw him off the bike at cornering speeds of over 100 mph. So we had to fit longer rear units with lighter spring loadings, and get more travel from the front forks, in order to soak up these undulations.

My first rider was Mick Andrew, who had all the natural talents, but not much experience. I liked his style when I saw him racing in that 1968 Barcelona event. He had his own 350 cc Aermacchi, but it became obvious to me that we would have to get new 350 and 500 cc machines so that he could gain more experience and maintain form, because you certainly cannot expect to mix it with the best if you don't get the racing miles under you. Now you can see what I mean by becoming involved!

Later, in 1969, I decided to enter the TT for the first time. Now, if you really want success in the Island you have to get yourself one of the tiny band of riders who are capable of lapping at over 100 mph. In my first attempt I almost got Malcolm Uphill, but Triumph offered him a better financial deal and I finished up with Tom Dickie, who gave me a third place in the Senior and fourth place in the Junior. Mick Andrew, the novice, came fourth in the production race, so I finished up well pleased with my debut in the Island.

I still think our best day's racing was at the 1972 Hutch, at Brands Hatch, when Dave Potter won the production event and the Mellano Trophy. The last race of the day was the Formula 750, in which we were placed fourth, sixth and eighth out of nine finishers. At the end of the day's racing, in which we had been out in every other event, including the 50-lap, 100-kilometre race, all the bikes were still running. Most of the works Nortons and Triumphs had dropped out, leaving only one of each team still in action.

I have always been interested in 24-hour events, as in my view they are an excellent way for a manufacturer to prove his product. This is true much more so than in short circuit racing, which is inclined to produce 'specials'. But in a long distance race a bike has to take punishment and keep going. If Nortons had shown an interest four years ago, listened to our views and taken the trouble to examine the parts that I returned to them I think they would not have had gearbox trouble on their John Player machines in 1972. It goes without saying that if a gearbox will stand 24 hours of racing it is a good component and will take everyday usage in its stride. The same thing holds true for the clutch.

The Norton gearbox in the Commando is a very good box of its type, and while it does an excellent job on a road machine it is not quite up to top class racing. In fact it is really on the limit. We need a stronger box and I would like to see it redesigned. The fact that no good shock absorber is incorporated in the transmission does not help. The result is that the pinions take a shock load hammering they could well do without. This has been the root cause of the trouble, which leads to broken teeth and locked-up gearboxes—a problem that does not endear itself to riders.

I have entered seven machines in 24-hour races, but finished in only one. We have always retired with gearbox failure, except once when Charlie Sanby fell off in 1971. We have

Vincent Davey talking tactics with rider Dave Potter . . .

. . . and sharing a joke with fellow sponsor Stan Shenton.

Charlie Sanby was one of the most successful Gus Kuhn riders, lapping the TT circuit at over 102 mph on one of the team's 750 cc Nortons.

never had to make any adjustment to an engine, despite the fact that on four occasions we lasted more than half distance. This speaks volumes for our engines—Jim certainly does a good job in this department and I can truthfully say we almost never get an oil leak from the motors. On the odd occasion when we do it is usually from the contact breaker oil seal.

I have had no special help from the Norton factory in the way of technical advice or special parts. I have gone my own way, which in one sense is a good thing. It teaches you to be self-sufficient, and now I honestly feel we know as much about racing as they do. After all, less than 25 per cent of the machine is Norton, the rest we get made or make ourselves. Our bikes do not compare too badly with factory machines, and what we lack in financial terms we make up for in enthusiasm and the experience of constant racing. However, that is not to say we could not do a lot more with a little more money in the kitty.

I often wonder what the attitude of the factories is to people like us, because on the one hand we do a good job for their publicity, but on the other hand it can be embarrassing for them if dealers who have to operate on very small budgets go out and beat them on the track!

A person who wants to go racing should be able to build a competitive machine with good tuning and preparation on a reasonable budget. I believe that my team fulfils a role in this context, as what we do could be achieved by anyone who wished to devote the time and money to it and accumulate the experience.

However, one is bound to reflect on the justice of having to race against works teams in production and Formula 750 events when the factories hold all the ace cards. Under the present rules, it is they who decide what equipment is allowed and what will be accepted and homologated. But I shouldn't complain, as the public expect the factory teams to win, and this makes it all the more impressive if we manage to beat them, as we have done on more than one occasion. At Silverstone in 1972 we beat the works Norton riders in every event they entered, including Jody Nicholas, who had been brought at great expense from America and was beaten fair and square by Dave Potter on a machine that was slower on top end speed, but was better set up for the circuit.

People often ask me: 'Who is the best rider you have ever had?' I suppose the correct answer is: 'The rider who is with me now'. After all, you must rate him, otherwise you would find someone else. I certainly think Dave Potter is as good as any of my previous riders, but they are really all so different.

I still think Dave Croxford is a great rider, and a real character, who still enjoys his racing and can be very fast when he wants to be. Pat Mahoney is very popular with all my family; his claim to fame with them is being the only rider who brought my wife flowers whenever he came to see us. Pat also, I think, still enjoys his racing but is very aware that it is only by asking for your just rewards that you stand any chance of getting them.

On the other hand, Charlie Sanby is a very serious rider. I sometimes wonder if he really enjoys his racing that much any more. But he really surprised everyone, including me, when he lapped the Island at 102 mph and was in second position on the last lap in the 1971 Formula 750 event, only to drop out with a bad connection on the battery. But that was Charlie—probably the most unlucky rider who ever rode for me. He always amazed me by going just as quickly as other riders five stone lighter. I still cannot work that one out.

I have already mentioned Mick Andrew. His death in a road accident in 1970 was a very great blow. He was a popular rider, intelligent and ambitious. In his first full year with me in 1969 he had 350 and 500 cc Kuhn Seeleys and a 750 cc production racer to use in the Island. That's giving a rider opportunities if you like! He had no real experience of the Isle of Man, and I know you cannot expect results first time, but he was my favourite rider then, and he worked for me in our workshop, so I wanted him to gain experience. I even took another customised production Commando for him to use to learn the 37¾-

At the meeting that marked the closure of the Crystal Palace circuit in 1972, Vincent Davey enjoys a lap on vintage machinery.

mile circuit in the periods between official practices when the roads were open. Charlie Sanby, his close friend, also went over with Mick especially to help him, as Charlie was not riding in the TT that year. Mick finished fourth in the Production event and lapped at over 96 mph on the bike, a speed that would have made him third in the 1972 Production TT. He came back a much better rider, and won the Hutch production event and the Grovewood award for the most improved rider of the year.

The controversy surrounding the TT during the past two years in my view stems completely from money. This was the reason I did not go with my machines in 1972. I simply could not afford the time and expense of almost two weeks of racing and practice. I reckon it costs me at least £400 to go there, so I chose to concentrate on other events, and I didn't regret it. I feel the same reasons motivate the professional riders who criticise the event. Pay them well and I am sure you will find they will put up with the dangers. One thing is for sure—if you want riding experience, the Island provides a type of racing that improves the standard of the rider and gives him a great fund of experience to draw upon. It also, of course, improves machine preparation, because it's a very tough circuit on the bike and with so much practice required, a lot of faults show up.

My respect for the TT as the supreme test of a road racer does not blind me to the necessity of a British Grand Prix circuit that would present itself to foreign riders as a more attractive proposition. One has to see the difficulty facing riders who would like to compete in the TT, but cannot spare the time needed to learn the circuit. There is also the expense and the fact that it is dangerous if you try to rush things. An alternative would be to have a British Grand Prix on a mainland circuit. I favour the Brands Hatch 2.65-mile long circuit for its facilities, ease of access from the Continent, and spectator accommodation. The circuit management have the experience to handle it professionally. This would be Britain's classic for world championship points, and not the TT.

I do not see why this should spell the end of the TT, as it could continue as a world-ranking event with trade support and sponsorship from interested parties. I think it could stand on its own merits as the supreme test of a rider's skill (even if it does favour the home product), and almost the most demanding in machine preparation.

It is the 24-hour races which undoubtedly place the greatest stresses on machine preparation, and I must say I really enjoy entering bikes in them. The first requirement with an endurance event is to prepare the bike to finish, so you must detune the engine slightly. You must also match the compression ratio to the fuel available. In Barcelona, for example, the best fuel you can get is 96 octane, so we bring the compression down to 9.8:1 for that race.

We try to ensure that nothing on the bike can work loose. Any components which could possibly break must be easily replaced, which is why you rarely see 24-hour bikes carrying full fairings. Electrical components must be duplicated, and the suspension must be softened to give the riders additional comfort. We also modify the riding position to give them room to stretch. A genuine racing crouch would be unbearable in a 24-hour event.

The work done in the pits is as important in the marathons as the racing on the track. Just look at any British short circuit race. If you get 30 starters, a dozen may well drop out in a 20-minute race. Now imagine the work that goes into preparing a bike that must last for 24 hours!

At one time I used to enter a team of two bikes in endurance races, but that was really beyond our resources, and now I've gone back to running a single machine. Dave Sleat, my racing mechanic, and I service the bike during the races, although I stick to the simpler tasks such as topping up the oil level and adjusting the rear brake. Dave is perfect as a mechanic for these events, because he is probably the swiftest worker you can find. Usually, we manage to find an additional helper to assist with general tasks, and my daughter Valerie does much of the lap scoring. We get no sleep during the entire race, and we record everything that happens to the bike—fuel and oil consumption, every adjustment that has to be made, and any troubles. It is all invaluable experience to draw on for future races.

I am often asked the question, 'Why do you do it all?' Firstly, I can assure you it is not for business reasons, although quite obviously one wants to get some commercial return out of sponsorship. I feel I have to justify my racing activities to my business conscience, when I consider the expense of tying up capital, my best workshop staff and valuable space. But the real enjoyment I get from sponsorship is the satisfaction of setting out to do something well and achieving it. If we have a good day and win races, I feel happy and elated—an obvious and normal reaction, but that's what it's all about. My main aim in racing is really to win, regardless of whether I beat the factory teams or other private entrants. I have never regarded the works bikes as unbeatable, and I think by now that I've been proved correct in that attitude.

CHAPTER 9

Far away
from the superbikes

by Dave Amos, leading Bantam racer and tuner

THE BANTAM RACING CLUB'S 125 cc Bantam formula is probably the finest compromise between cost control and the building of a competitive racing motorcycle yet achieved in road racing. Irrespective of the money available to the prospective competitor, a little over £200 is the maximum he can intelligently spend without wasting his capital. Yet the result can be a machine that, given a good rider, can not only be capable of winning the Bantam Racing Club's Formula Bantam Championship, but can prove highly competitive in 125 cc racing at club level.

National and international success is not unusual. For example, the 1972 125 cc TT saw a fine 12th place by Mike Scutt on Robbie Winstone's Bantam, showing that given the right day (a very wet one in this case) the Bantam can compare with machines priced at four times its own cost.

The Bantam Racing Club's 125 cc formula is only restrictive in the following items:

1. Maximum capacity 125 cc;
2. The following engine and gearbox modifications not allowed:
   a) Mechanically forced oil feed;
   b) Induction other than piston controlled;
   c) Pressurised fuel injection (note that fuel injection by gravity or engine vacuum is allowed);
   d) Non BSA type gears (but pattern gears are allowed);
   e) Not more than three speeds;
   f) Non-standard cylinder barrel (but the standard barrel may be modified);
3. The Bantam frame loop must be incorporated in the frame design. The loop may be modified by sawing, filing and welding. Acceptance of modified frame is at the discretion of the committee;
4. Petrol tank must have a minimum capacity of one gallon and be mounted in the normal BSA Bantam position;
5. Fuel to be petrol only;
6. Sprockets to be of steel;
7. No stands, road number plates or standard BSA footrests allowed;
8. ACU standing regulations for road racing machines apply where necessary.

Analysing the formula, you will see that expensive frames are pointless, as the main loop, the heart of the frame, must be the original BSA component—so forget the expensive ultra-lightweight substitute. However, a light, good steering machine can be built by modifying the subframe, lengthening the swinging arm, and using well-balanced rear units and stiff lightweight forks. The machine's appearance can be improved by the use of a small slim tank and seat in glass fibre and a slim fairing that maximises rider and machine streamlining.

Let us continue our analysis of the engine. The Bantam crankcases must be used together with the BSA-type three-speed gearbox, thus disallowing expensive 'one off' crankcases and multi-speed gearboxes. Pricey modifications to the induction system are not allowed and one must use the basic cast iron BSA barrel. No alloy barrels are allowed either sleeved or incorporating a chrome-plated bore. Power can be improved by part modifications: high compression, squish, cylinder heads, racing pistons and stiff, small diameter, highly accurate crankshafts. Any type of spark generation is allowed and there are no carburettor restrictions. Finally, any exhaust system can be used.

When designing and modifying, the power characteristics should be made such that a usable power band is available, considering the limitations of the three-speed gearbox. This tends to bring out the best in tuning, machine building and riding. It also leads to a degree of ingenuity unparalleled in club racing. Running clearances must be minimised, yet power loss through friction should be avoided at the crankshaft, piston and cylinder head, and gearbox. The machine builder considers the power available and prepares his bike to maximise the power-to-weight ratio. The centre of gravity should be as close to the track as possible, but still allowing for the required angle of lean under all suspension conditions. He makes his rider as comfortable and streamlined in the riding position as possible.

The builder finally ensures that the maximum power is transmitted from the engine and realised at the rear wheel by reducing all sources of friction and drag at chains and wheels. The whole plot must steer well, remembering that the means of achieving the best results from a Bantam is to keep the power on through the corners, since fierce acceleration is not available with only a three-speed gearbox.

Formula Bantam racers leave the grid during a Snetterton meeting.

The best basis for a 125 cc Formula Bantam racer is a 175 cc frame. This can be obtained by closely watching small advertisements for a machine less engine, tank, seat and mudguards—never pay more than £15. The main frame loop has to be retained, according to the formula, but frame strengthening and lowering of the rear subframe is essential, as too is lengthening of the swinging arm. The majority of riders carry out this work themselves at minimal cost—rarely will these modifications exceed £15.

The standard 175 cc forks should be shortened 2½ inches, rebushed and the oil seals renewed, at a total cost of around £3. Brakes must be reshod and it is advisable to fit 18-inch alloy rims. Total cost here is about £30. New rear dampers, balanced, will set you back £8. Tank, seat and fairing will cost around £30 for a smart, functional combination set.

A used late 125 cc engine is the best start for the power unit, and I see no reason why the cost should exceed £10. The large, somewhat agricultural crankshaft should be changed for a racing component featuring 4-inch flywheels, a racing con-rod assembly and a short timing side shaft. To convert the inside diameter of the crankcases to 4 in, packing rings are used. The crankshaft and rings will be exchanged for £29. For a racing piston, cylinder head, carburettor, replacement oil seals and bearings, budget for £20.

You can have your barrel tuned by a specialist for £15. Close ratio gears and a four-plate clutch involves a further £30, and converting the ignition system to coil and battery will cost £10. For various incidentals add £25. So the cost of your new Bantam racer, ready for assembly, totals approximately £240, but a discount of 10 per cent can usually be obtained, reducing your cost to £216. Close scrutiny of small advertisements for certain second-hand parts may well effect a further saving of up to £50. This reduces your cost to

Brothers Dave (left) and Trevor Amos examine the barrel assembly of one of their racing Bantams.

£166. A further £25 could be saved if you have average engineering knowledge and ability, with access to welding and turning facilities and some engineering equipment. This, together with shrewd scrutiny of the spares market, means your Bantam racer need cost no more than £140!

The costs listed here are for a highly sophisticated machine capable, with good riding and preparation, of being among the leaders in 125 cc Formula Bantam racing. But a rider whose appetite is satisfied by performing in the lower echelons of Bantam racing can build a machine for infinitely less than £100. Similar costs to those I have mentioned will be incurred in building a 175 cc racing Bantam.

Generally a 125 Bantam is capable of being tuned to give 18 bhp, and a 175 to develop about 23 bhp.

So you have a machine—but what will you need in cash terms to race it?

The spares required for a normal season's racing—say ten meetings, involving 30 races—will rarely cost more than £30. Given a fair run of good fortune, the total will be less. At club level, a race entry will cost fractionally over £1 and insurance for a day will come to just under £1. So a day's racing, involving practice and three races, costs little more than £4. You can, therefore, race your Bantam with the Bantam Racing Club or with John Milligan's excellent British Formula Club for around £70 a year. For this you enjoy 30 races and maybe pick up a pot or two into the bargain.

You may be wondering how these machines perform. Kid yourself not—the racing Bantam is no sluggard. For speed comparisons, let us use the 2.71-mile Snetterton circuit as a base. Snetterton is a well organised circuit, has a long back straight, left and right hand bends, one acute hairpin, and slight gradients.

Considering the three-speed gearbox on a Bantam, the selection of suitable gearing is essential and a compromise must be found between acceleration, selection of the right gear for the various corners and gradients, and finally, maximum speed. You could gear for maximum speed for the straight but find the gearing incorrect for some corners, causing either over-revving or running below the rev-band. Naturally, correct gearing becomes increasingly critical as the number of gear speeds available decreases. On a still, fine day at Snetterton it is not unusual for the fastest 125 cc Formula Bantam machine to be operating on a gear ratio that gives 10 mph per 1,000 rpm in top gear.

Let me take you round a typical competitive flying lap of Snetterton on a 125 cc Bantam. Past the pits and over the finishing line the circuit is straight and rises slightly. I am flat on the tank trying to keep all I can inside the streamlining—an elbow in the breeze will knock off 100 rpm. The motor peaks at 8,000 rpm at the approach to Riches, a bumpy right hand corner. Touch the brakes to steady the bike, line up and take it in top, eyes peering over the top of the screen. Chin on the tank before straightening up for the dash to Sears—another right hand corner, approached at 8,000 rpm (or 80 mph). Sit up, change to second, take Sears at 8,000 in second. Flat on the tank and take the engine up to 10,500 and change into top for the straight. Through the left hand kink, again flat out, well tucked into the fairing.

Maximum revs of around 10,000 are seen about one-third the way down the straight. The bike is now doing 100 mph. Count the hairpin warning signs—500 yds, 400, 300, 200, wait—sit up, change twice, braking like hell. On the exit from the hairpin, get down again, change up two gears progressing down the home straight and peaking at 9,000 (90 mph). Touch the brakes for the Esses inside the 100 yard marker, feather the throttle a little, keep in top at 7,500, and take the left hander passing under the bridge, keeping the head well down. Quickly swing to the right and clip the grass on the exit, while flat on the tank. Keep wide for Coram Curve—a long bumpy right hander. Look for the right line, go over the well known bump there, and lean into Coram, close to the inside bank. The rev counter reads 7,500 as I start the drop for Russells. The short distance sees the revs rise to 8,000.

Looking as stylish as any rider on a £1,000 Yamaha, Dave Amos sweeps his 190 cc Bantam through a right-hander.

Russell is a nasty left and right hand, a narrow chicane with a small kerb. To get the best from the Bantam for the rise past the pits, I keep in top and take it at about 7,500. Then it's past the pits and into another lap.

I reckon I need certifying, squeezing my six foot frame into that streamlining and enjoying it. Taking corners at speeds the Post Office never knew existed and coming back for more must show some kind of bent tendency! So with me you have completed a lap of Snetterton in about 2 minutes 5 seconds, giving an average speed of just under 80 mph, with a maximum of around 100 mph.

About four Bantams are capable of 100 mph, and some six combinations of machine and rider are able to average 80 mph at Snetterton. At the opposite end of the scale, the novice grade lap record at Snetterton is just over 70 mph.

Strangely enough, very few people have attempted to build a 175 cc Bantam racer yet, based upon the four-speed BSA D14/4, an excellent machine can be built capable of speeds of up to 108 mph. A well prepared cycle will prove to be extremely competitive with the average club 250, and will often score on reliability. Looking back on our lap of Snetterton, you will be aware of the importance of tidy riding: head down, knees and elbows out of the slipstream, all corners taken as fast as possible, maintaining the engine revs in the power band. Even considering the most sophisticated Bantam, the available power is so very small that the only means of obtaining good results is by intelligent, tidy, fast riding.

The Bantam Racing Club organises and promotes race meetings and social functions primarily for Bantam racers. To provide variety, production machine, 250 cc and unlimited classes are catered for at the ten or so race meetings organised each season. Racing membership stands at around 400 members, about half of whom are active Bantam racers. But organised Formula Bantam events are held by many other clubs. Northern Ireland, not catered for by the Bantam Racing Club, is the scene of some keen interest in racing Bantams of all capacities, performing in the popular 200 cc handicaps. But although many senior clubs are happy to see Bantams among their entries, the Bantam Racing Club is still the Mecca of Bantam racing, providing the fiercest and fastest competition.

Rider grading is the key to the good, safe and fast formula racing of the Bantam Racing Club. There are three grades of 125 cc Bantam rider—novice, intermediate and senior. A competitor is regarded as a novice until he has won any road race. He is then promoted to intermediate and remains in that grade until he wins any of the club's 125 cc races, other than the novice event. He is then considered a senior rider. At the end of a season's racing all senior riders, except the championship's top 12, revert to intermediate grade.

The club's 125 cc race programme is divided into novice races (for novices only), intermediate/novice races (for both grades of rider), and championship events, which count towards the 125 cc Bantam championship. Any grade of rider may enter, but priority is given to senior riders. There are also open events, for all grades of rider. An important annual event is the Snetterton Enduro meeting. This incorporates hour-long races for all classes, and is a real test of reliability. Occasionally additional events are held for all 125 cc machines to provide a comparison for riders against foreign bikes. Bantams have often recorded good wins in these.

The 175 cc Bantams have an airing in the 250 cc events. Provided there are more than three 175 cc Bantams starting, trophies are awarded. Surprisingly enough, there is only one regular competitor, and that is the 190 cc Bantam run by my brother Trevor and me. I say surprisingly, because a well-prepared 175 is competitive at club level. The club hold meetings at a variety of circuits. All are chosen to achieve good close competition at minimum cost. The venues are:—

SNETTERTON, NORFOLK: Almost three miles in length, good surface, left and right hand bends, one hairpin, gradients and a very long straight. This circuit brings out the best in machine speed and reliability.

CADWELL PARK, LINCS: Charles Wilkinson's beautiful circuit. The 1.3-mile club circuit is used, incorporating a very good surface, left and right hand bends, one hairpin, medium length straight and acute gradients. You need a tidy rider and a machine with good all-round performance.

LLANDOW, S WALES: One mile round, poor surface, right hand bends only, no hairpin and two short straights incorporating slight gradients. A circuit that demands brave riding and a good handling machine.

LYDDEN, KENT: One mile circuit with a fair surface, both right and left hand bends, one hairpin, only a very short straight, but quite acute gradients.

Two of the circuits mentioned are eminently suitable for Bantam racers. More than one very slow corner takes the emphasis away from good brave riding and swings it to acceleration and multi-speed gearboxes.

The BSA Bantam road machine is now dead, but the Bantam racer still flourishes and performance mproves as each season progresses. The legendary reliability of the BSA Bantam has been built into the 125 cc and 175 cc racers, but do remember that the 125 cc formula still does not permit the use of the excellent late Bantam four-speed gearbox or alloy barrels. BSA have available the basis for a successful range of 125 cc, 175 cc and 200 cc single-cylinder two-stroke machines with an existing sporting image.

The following items are required: the four-speed crankcase and gearbox; racing type 4 inch stiff crankshaft; an alloy line barrel; D14/4 type thin ring piston but incorporating steel rings and a squish type cylinder head; finally, a universal frame similar to our own 190, being duplex, light and very manageable.

Private enterprise and the Bantam Racing Club are ensuring that spares are available for the racing Bantams, and I forsee many more years of Bantam racing even without renewed interest from BSA. The present formula is exceptionally sound. This is borne out by the continuing interest still shown in Bantam racing. The enthusiasm still borders on the fanatical, performances improve and the Bantam Racing Club's finances are sound. This is a good position to reflect upon what is required of a formula to bring racing to the pocket of the apprentice and the 'semi-detached' family man.

The average enthusiast can usually muster about £200 capital to spend on the machine (without selling his wife into slavery or mortgaging the council house). With a standard of living bordering on the monastic, he can find an average of £5 a week to dedicate to racing. Right, we have tremendous enthusiasm, £200 capital and a potential £250 for expenses. Our friend is about to embark upon a career in racing that, he hopes, will be second only in success to that achieved by a certain Stanley Michael Bailey Hailwood (what a shame you have only one Christian name).

Assuming transport is available in the form of a car, trailer or van, riding gear has to be purchased. For this first hole in our £200 capital, say £50, do not skimp, but get some sound stuff and not too flashy. Gold leathers and red boots look great when you are first past the flag, but awfully conspicuous when you're lapped. They will also get very tatty after an hour on your knees in the paddock trying to set up a machine whose parentage you doubt.

Now only £150 is left for the bike. The dealer has a beautiful 250 for £150 down and only £5 per week, but then if you take it there is no money left to run the bike (the wife has already locked the kids' piggy bank away so forget that). So our first restriction is that the bike should be available for about £150. Spares, transportation and racing fees must come from the £250 per year. The average racing appetite is satisfied with around 50 races per year—say 18 meetings. Remember most clubs operate six- to eight-lap races (the Bantam Club's are eight laps) at an average of £1.50 per race, including insurance. Fees

Engine department: Trevor Amos' 175 cc Bantam.

then, are £75 per year. Travelling to meetings is the next significant expense. An average day will involve around 250 miles, unless you live close to a circuit and restrict your activities to that one alone. Budget for £100 per year.

You have £75 left for spares, replacement riding gear and other incidentals. Therefore, spares must be cheap and readily available. So the formula must be based upon a simple road machine. No racing is enjoyed permanently on your knees in the paddock or pushing in past wags in the stand. The vast majority of club racers prepare their own machines. This demands simplicity, and single-cylinder two-strokes are eminently suitable.

Fairness in the formula rules must be seen to operate. Restrictions on engine modification must be those that are visibly apparent. It is no use disallowing internal modifications if these changes cannot be easily scrutinised by officials and fellow competitors alike. Therefore, formulae that insist on the use of standard engines without modifications would be unworkable.

The image is important. The formula must allow the machine to look like a racer. Insistence upon standard tanks, seats and, today, no streamlining, spells doom. The formula must also give everyone an equal chance of success and ensure close racing—even for the rank novice. This means grading—novices to race against novices for their own trophies, experts to be in their own class too. Incidentally, handicaps never really prove satisfactory or safe.

So what is the basis for a formula? The machine must be purchased at a cost below £200 and provide reliability by nature of its design. It must be possible to prepare it at home with the minimum of specialised equipment. Total spares must cost no more than £100 a year for an intelligently prepared machine. The formula must allow visible scrutiny of machine specifications, and yet the bikes must look like modern racers. Finally, there is no future in a formula that increases the danger of racing through insistence upon the use of inadequate or badly placed components, or handicapping.

I think you will agree that the Bantam formula meets all these requirements.

Bantam racing is close: here Peter Styles leads Mick Scutt.

CHAPTER 10

The future for road racing

by Neville Goss, a member of the FIM's technical committee and the ACU's competitions committee

---

NO ONE CAN HOPE to gaze into a crystal ball and project the exact pattern the sport will follow in the years to come. To be gifted with such magical powers would indeed be worth a fortune. What can be done is to take a look at present trends and to assess the manner in which they could develop.

Road racing falls into two distinct categories; racing on courses which are true roads with all the natural features of a public highway; and racing circuits specially constructed with all the accompanying facilities to provide, not only a venue for competitive racing, but additionally all the requirements of an outdoor public entertainment centre.

Few of the road racing circuits now remain. The Isle of Man TT course is without doubt the greatest of them all. This and Northern Ireland's Dundrod, West Germany's Nurburgring, Opatija in Yugoslavia and the Czech GP course at Brno, are probably the best known remaining examples of a sport that has existed now for more than half a century. It is doubtful if this number will ever be increased. Modern trends in highway construction and traffic requirements would never permit it. For this reason it is vital that these circuits must be preserved, not as legacies of the past, but because of the inestimable value that they possess as a contribution to the future. To race successfully upon them represents the ultimate in riding skill. The exacting nature of such a course leads to the essential and more rapid development of better motorcycles, not only in engine performance but additionally in brakes, steering, handling and comfort—the last named an essential factor in reducing rider fatigue.

The future for these circuits is fully assured and success on them will become of even greater importance both to the riders and also to manufacturers.

On the other hand, the specially constructed circuits are wholly dependent for their future upon finance and the ability of their owners to provide worth-while entertainment for the paying public. Provided this can be continually improved, their future is secure. But it is this responsibility, which rests wholly upon the circuit owners, of ensuring that the public receive value for money that controls this section of the sport. It becomes much more a question of financial investment than a pastime. There is already a conflict of interests here which arises when a circuit cannot exist solely for motorcycle racing but must cater for car racing as well.

Not the least of these problems is the question of rider safety. There exists in the car world at the moment an obsession for Armco barriers fringing the course at every conceivable point. There is no doubt the barriers provide valuable protection for the spectating public, but also create an enormous hazard for competitors not only on two wheels, but those on four as well. A car striking the barrier is invariably thrown back on to the circuit directly into the path of following vehicles and what was initially one car leaving the circuit becomes a two or three car heap of wreckage in the middle of the course. Furthermore, the effect of a vehicle laden with high octane fuel striking a metal barrier provides a considerable fire hazard.

A more satisfactory means of providing protection between motorcyclists and spectators must and will be sought. Wherever metal barriers exist they must be padded during motorcycle meetings. Already there are indications that plastic-covered rubber foam or glass-fibre wool can provide suitable protection in place of the emergency precaution of straw bales. While bales provide a reasonable measure of safety, they can only be regarded as a temporary expedient. Ideally the situation should be resolved by the removal of metal barriers and their replacement by a vertical protective chalk bank and a running off space of loose shingle, which would provide a rapid deceleration medium for all vehicles out of control.

Rider protection is quite a different matter when racing takes place on closed public roads. The risks are greater and a rider is conscious of these, which is just one of the reasons why he always produces his best, his most skilled and polished performance when competing on them. It is just not possible to eliminate every hazard around a true road course any more than it is possible to erect a safety net at the base of the Matterhorn. What

Neville Goss, organiser of the Southampton club's 500-mile production race at Thruxton, congratulates 1972 winners Dave Croxford (left) and Mick Grant. They rode the works 750 cc Norton Commando.

can be done is to study these circuits and to minimise the risk at any obvious danger points. The easing of difficult corners and bends, the provision of running-off spaces following these bends and the creation of unobstructed slip roads at points where brake failure could spell serious trouble are some of the features which a specially appointed track inspection panel of the FIM looked at when they visited every grand prix circuit before the 1973 season.

Noise is another problem affecting the future development of racing circuits. Here again, much of this criticism stems from the indiscriminate use of unsilenced cars. However, it

Neville Goss would like to see a full F750 world championship. Short circuit clashes like this one between Cal Rayborn (Harley-Davidson, 3) and Ray Pickrell (Triumph) might then be repeated on GP circuits.

Le Mans-type start at a Brands Hatch 500-mile production race.

must be frankly admitted that the sound emitted from an unsilenced multi-cylinder two-stroke motorcycle on full chat is anything but musical.

There is little doubt that the silencing of all forms of motorcycle and car racing vehicles must and will come. It will probably start in the car world and motorcyclists will be compelled to follow suit. We have seen its half-hearted enforcement in this country in the sphere of moto cross and already Europe is beginning to follow suit. Soon we can look forward to an international standard of maximum noise levels for all forms of racing.

Generally, manufacturers will welcome this for it will enable them to produce machines to one standard instead of varying them between one market and another. There will be objections, of course. The Italians are already on record as saying that the public needs noise to create a racing atmosphere and without it public support would fade. Against this, there is production machine racing in this country when full road silencing is obligatory and the favourable comments of supporters who delight in being able to carry out a normal conversation whilst racing is in progress.

Since the end of the Second World War road race meetings in Britain have fallen into three categories—international, national and club. The public demand for improved entertainment on the short circuits has brought about the increasing development of international meetings. Some 20 years ago these were dominated by British riders and British machines and the appearance of a foreign name in the programme was invariably nothing more than a gesture which served to indicate the status of the meeting.

Today this has changed considerably. The recession in the British motorcycle industry and the subsequent growth in importance of foreign manufacturers has produced foreign riders of a calibre comparable with our own. The process is accelerating rapidly as more and more overseas short circuits are developed. It is not surprising, therefore, that one looks for top-line foreign representation at British international meetings today.

But to bring more foreigners to this country from greater distances must increase promotional costs. Promoters will in future be reluctant to take risks involving a heavy financial outlay and will look more and more for a secure monetary return. There will be a reduction in early and late season meetings, which run foul of the unpredictable British spring and autumn weather. Instead, we can look for a selective but smaller number of meetings arranged throughout our all-too-brief summer on weekends when there are no counter attractions abroad or world championship rounds.

At the other end of the scale club racing is at present on the crest of a wave of popularity. It should continue in this vein all the time that newcomers to the sport are waiting to learn and to progress to more ambitious spheres. Club racing today is financed almost entirely by the riders themselves. They do not profess to provide first class public entertainment, but it is in such activities that we find the competitor who is racing just for the pleasure he obtains from it.

The problem with this wealth of talent now being demonstrated and developed at club level is: what steps can a rider take in order to graduate beyond this sphere? The logical step should be to events of national level, but this is where the pattern of British road racing fixtures is sadly lacking. There are national meetings, but some are little better than club meetings. And in the same way, some club meetings are often national in character. Certainly riders are no longer drawn from the geographical neighbourhood of the promoting club. Often they are encouraged to travel considerable distances either by the attraction of financial reward or, more frequently, by the quality of organisation and the opportunity to gain further experience at a particular circuit.

Turning to Formula 750, this class was first introduced to this country in 1971, to enable the two major British companies—BSA-Triumph and Norton—to pursue a racing policy which would give them the chance to compete both in this country and in their major export market, America, under a common set of regulations.

Neville Goss is an ardent supporter of public roads circuits such as the TT course. But Phil Read, pictured here rounding Ballacraine on the 350 MV, is an outspoken critic of the Mountain circuit.

The basic principle of Formula 750, which limits major engine components to those used in the construction of series production models, is good, because it helps to keep the cost of manufacturer participation in racing within reasonable limits. It also eliminates the use of a laboratory produced racing prototype built with infinite precision regardless of cost to provide maximum publicity. These costs invariably force a company to disappear from the scene as soon as the commercial advantage has been obtained. This leaves a temporary void in racing circles until another manufacturer comes along with a similar idea.

Up to this point, Formula 750 is beneficial and is understood throughout Europe. Unfortunately, it goes on to control many other features of the motorcycle's design and construction, including frames, brakes, suspension, and even fuel tanks, by requiring prior approval for their use from the engine manufacturer concerned. This may be all very well for America, where there is no national motorcycle industry, but only a distribution network for predominantly foreign products. It is, however, a very progressive network which readily understands the supreme importance of the sport as a publicity medium to increase sales. In consequence, the controlling bodies of the sport and the trade enjoy a unique measure of co-operation with one another. It would be quite unfair to suggest that either one controls the other. But what one can say is that many leading personalities on one side also hold important appointments on the other.

Formula 750 should stop at its engine requirements, leaving all other components to the free choice of the individual. It could then form the basis of a single solo world road racing championship, replacing the present multiplicity of 50, 125, 250, 350 and 500 cc classes. A supplementary 250 cc class could also be run, and the sidecar world championship would

Giacomo Agostini signs autographs after winning another TT, but there is no victory smile. Ago also condemns the Mountain circuit as too dangerous.

Agostini bumps the MV into life in the 1972 TT. By the end of that week, he had lapped the TT course at over 100 mph no less than 53 times, a record achievement.

be retained. Additionally, the advent of Formula 750 in the world championships should attract and retain greater manufacturer interest; and there is no doubt that the active participation of manufacturers not only enhances these events, but provides considerable marketing benefits for the factories as well. What must be avoided in future is the start-stop policy adopted for commercial reasons by manufacturers at the present time. The best way is to provide a formula which will keep racing costs within reasonable limits.

Finance, more than any other subject, dominates the world championships today; not only with manufacturers, but to an even greater degree with riders. Riders tend to believe, sometimes quite justifiably, that Continental grands prix are big money-spinners for the promoters. At the same time, some competitors have inflated notions of their own value, and make excessive demands for starting money. The promoter, on the other hand, thinks that a rider cannot afford to miss a world championship meeting and not unnaturally tries to obtain his services for as little as possible.

What we must remember is that while we have paid riders—and in some instances they are paid very handsomely indeed—the great majority of officials at meetings are volunteers. But one cannot help wondering just how long they will continue freely to give of their time and experience, and involve themselves in personal expense, in order to provide star riders with a glamorous livelihood.

Until now the FIM has regarded the question of finance as a matter for negotiation between rider and promoter, but the indications are that this situation will not be allowed to continue for much longer. The international body will probably produce a scale of minimum payment which must be made to riders at world championship meetings. This could be based on a rider's previous performances. No doubt a rider's position or the points he has gained in the previous year's world championships will form the initial basis for such an assessment. This does not help a newcomer to the series, but this problem could be overcome if each country was allowed to nominate an additional one or two riders each year. They would qualify for a scale of payment equivalent to a low championship position in the previous year. This would be an extra benefit for the British championship title-holder.

Measures are already in hand to adopt a zoning policy for world championship events in order to reduce the amount of travelling to an acceptable level. This involves a complete rescheduling of the traditional dates of classic meetings. Events will be held in adjoining countries on consecutive weekends, and free weekends will allow for machine maintenance and travel when competitors move from one zone to another.

Currency problems for Iron Curtain countries may cause the East German and Czech events to disappear, but there is little prospect of any other method of reducing championship rounds being used at the moment. In fact, each member country has a right to organise a grand prix, although it does not automatically count as a world championship event. It could well be that the number of grands prix will increase, and it will certainly not be long before there is one in America. What the FIM will probably do is to hold the number of events in which a rider can score points to its present maximum of seven, or even reduce it to six, with three in each half of the season. At the same time it may reduce the number of championship classes. This would give a rider a wider choice of events from which he can choose to contest the championship.

Whatever the FIM does you may rest assured that its progress will be extremely slow. In fact, one gathers the impression that this international governing body takes decisions which will affect posterity rather than the immediate future. In some respects this is understandable, for it holds a full meeting only once a year, and always insists upon planning events two and three years ahead. Even so, it is often too slow to arrive at decisions, faced as it is with a multiplicity of languages and divergent national customs and ideas.

One factor that is certain, however, is that the FIM's member nations are still considerably influenced by the success or otherwise of racing developments in Great Britain. The moral of this must be, if you wish to influence the FIM in any way, first demonstrate your ideas successfully in your own country.

In production machine racing, endurance events have developed as a special sphere of activity. The early problems of production machine specifications, when competitors would modify machines to obtain some slight advantage, have now virtually been overcome in England. Strict enforcement of the rules, coupled with firm and efficient scrutineering, has achieved a state of affairs which is admired by many European countries. There is no doubt that the FIM would like to move closer to the British form of production racing. To do so, however, means that British methods of applying regulations would have to be enforced at all foreign international meetings, and I do not believe that the rest of Europe is ready for this yet.

The probable development will be that all events counting for the FIM Coupe d'Endurance will, within a few years, be run under the present British production rules. This will set the required standard in three or four countries, one of which would certainly not be France, for the total disregard for FIM rules at times displayed by the French will cause them to develop their own 24-hour Bol d'Or into a unique event open to any class of machine, provided it is equipped with lights.

Endurance events in other countries—and there are four at present with Britain, Belgium, Holland and Spain as organisers—have already reached the stage where entries are oversubscribed. The popularity of such events must create a demand for more in other countries and this is likely to be met within a very short time, for in this type of racing one gets nearer to the spirit of team racing for sport than in any other sphere.

Leading riders

Giacomo Agostini

BORN 1943 at Lovere, Italy. Started racing in Italian hill-climbs on a 175 Morini, and later won works support from the factory. Joined MV in 1965 and scored his first GP victory in the 350 cc West German classic that year. Since then he has taken the 350 and 500 cc MVs to ten TT victories, and has recorded 53 laps at over 100 mph on the Isle of Man—a record total. Winner of 12 world championships.

Art Baumann

BORN 1944. His most famous achievement is not winning a race, but being the world's fastest officially timed road racer at 171.75 mph, a speed he attained during qualifying for the 1972 Daytona 200, on the works 750 cc Suzuki. A Californian, he never rode a motorcycle until he was 21, but progressed rapidly after entering racing on a 350 Honda. In 1967 he became a works Yamaha rider in America, and in 1969, on a 500 cc works Suzuki, he became the first man to win an AMA 'national' on a two-stroke, in the Sears Point road race.

Mark Brelsford

BORN 1949. Top amateur rider in America in 1968. Joined Harley-Davidson in 1969, when he graduated to expert status. Won the American Motorcycle Association's No 1 plate in 1972, when he also won three 'nationals'. A brilliant rider on mile dirt tracks, he also gave Harley's new XR750 alloy engine its first victory, on the Louisville half-mile in 1972.

Kel Carruthers

BORN 1938. A major figure in international road racing, his brilliant career has led him from his home country of Australia, to works rides in Europe, and now to America. Winner of the 1969 and 1970 250 cc TTs, he also won the 1969 250 cc world title on the works Benelli-4. Left Europe in 1970 to live in America, and in 1971 he won six of the seven AMA 250 cc races on Don Vesco's Yamahas. On a factory 350 Yamaha he finished second to John Cooper's BSA by only six inches at the Ontario classic in 1971.

Derek Chatterton

BORN 1945. Started racing at 16 on a KTT Velocette, and later became the first rider to win the 250 and 350 cc British championships on two-stroke machines. Won the 250 cc title in 1967, and the 350 cc championship in 1970, both on Yamahas. A garage owner from Sibsey, Lincs, he prepares his own machines. Riding his 350 Yamaha, he beat Agostini into second place in the 1,000 cc race at Cadwell Park in September 1971.

John Cooper

BORN in Derby 1938, where he now runs a garage and Yamaha racing service. Won a race in his first meeting, on a 197 cc James at Osmaston Manor, Derbyshire, in 1954. Renowned for his dry wit and outspoken comments, Cooper had to wait until 1971 before he got his first major factory ride, on the 750 cc BSA-3. On the BSA, he scored his greatest successes when he beat Giacomo Agostini and the 500 cc MV in the 1971 Race of the Year, and a few weeks later won over £6,000 at Ontario, California, in the Champion Spark Plug Classic. Joined Nortons for 1973.

Klaus Enders

BORN 1937. Brilliant West German who came out of retirement from motorcycling in 1972 to take the sidecar world championship on a new monocoque BMW. Also won the 1967, '69 and '70 world titles. Winner of the 1969 and '70 500 cc sidecar TTs, and still the absolute sidecar lap record holder on the Isle of Man at 94.32 mph, a speed standing since 1968.

Mick Grant

BORN 1944. Began racing on a 250 cc Cotton scrambler, then turned to road racing in 1967 on a 500 cc Velocette. On the Velo, he finished 48th and last in the 1968 Senior Manx GP. On Padgett Yamaha and Kawasaki machines, he finished third in both the 1972 Junior and Senior TTs, with a fastest lap a fraction under the 'ton', at 99.95 mph. Earned a John Player Norton contract in 1972, and gave the factory its first win in the MCN Superbike series, at Scarborough. 1972 British 350 cc champion on a Padgett Yamaha.

Yvon du Hamel

BORN 1941. Tiny (5 ft 1 in) French Canadian with a reputation as the wildest and most forceful rider on American circuits. Won the 250 cc race at Daytona in 1968 and '69 on Yamahas, and won the 1971 Talladega 200 at 108.46 mph after joining Kawasaki. Won the 1972 125-miler at Road Atlanta on the Team Hansen 750 Kawasaki. Made his British debut in the 1970 Race of the Year, when he finished 10th on a 350 Yamaha. Won the 1972 Talladega 200, on the 750 Kawasaki, at 110.441 mph.

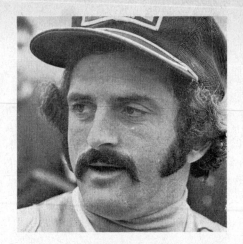

Norman Hanks

BORN 1944. With Chris Vincent's departure for the GPs in 1972, Hanks took over as the leading British short circuit sidecar rider, and won the British championship. Started racing in AMCA sidecar scrambling at 15 on a 600 cc ES2 Norton, and entered road racing a year later on father Fred's Norton outfit. As a member of the BSA competition shop, he worked as a mechanic for the factory GP moto cross team in 1968, '69 and '70. Second in the first ever 750 cc sidecar TT in 1968, and third in the British sidecar championships in 1969, '70 and '71, always on his BSA outfits.

Tony Jefferies

BORN 1948. A Yorkshire motorcycle dealer, Jefferies began racing in 1967 at Croft on a 500 cc Triumph. Won his first international at Scarborough in 1970. The toast of the Isle of Man in 1971 when he won the first-ever Formula 750 TT on a Triumph, the Junior race on a Yamaha, and placed second in the Production race on a Triumph. Twice chosen to race in the Anglo-American match races.

Steve Machin

BORN 1945. A garage proprietor from Wragby, Lincolnshire, he started racing in 1965 on a 200 cc Triumph Tiger Cub, and scored his first win on the bike before switching to a 250 cc Greeves Silverstone in 1966. Scored his first national and international wins in the same race, the 125 cc event at Cadwell in 1968, on a Bultaco. Most famous for his racing on his self-prepared Yamahas. British 250 cc champion in 1970, '71 and '72, and 125 cc champion in 1972.

Dick Mann

BORN 1934. Probably the world's most versatile racing motorcyclist. Equally at home on dirt tracks or road circuits. A professional racer for 20 years, he won the American Motorcycle Association championship in 1963 and '71, and finished second in '59, '64, and '65. Winner of the Daytona 200 in 1970 on a Honda and in 1971 on a BSA. Best American rider in the 1971 Anglo-American match races.

Charles Mortimer

BORN 1949. Won his first race at Brands Hatch in 1966, a year after he started racing. An ex-public schoolboy, he became a pupil and later an instructor at the road racing school once run by his father, Charles Snr. Won the 1970 250 cc Production TT on a Ducati, and a year later won the 125 cc TT on his debut ride with a works Yamaha. Also won the 1972 125 TT, again on a Yamaha. Third in 1972 125 cc world championship.

Angel Nieto

BORN 1947. Fiery little Spaniard who won his first GP in the 50 cc class of the 1969 East German round, on a Derbi. Went on to become 50 cc world champion in 1969 and 1970. Winner of two 125 cc world titles on the Derbi two-stroke twin against tough opposition. In 1971 he beat off Barry Sheene and Gilberto Parlotti, and in 1972 he beat Charles Mortimer and Borje Jansson. Also won the '72 50 cc world title.

Ray Pickrell

BORN 1938. A process engraver from London, he started racing in 1961 on a 500 cc Manx Norton. A brilliant specialist in big capacity machinery, he has never bothered to turn professional or attack the world championships. Winner of four TTs —the 1968, '71 and '72 Production races, and the '72 Formula 750 event with a record lap at 105.68 mph on the Triumph Trident. The only man to beat Californian Cal Rayborn in the 1972 Anglo-American match races. Suffered serious injuries in a crash at Mallory Park late in 1972.

Dave Potter

BORN 1950. Won the 750 cc British championship in 1972 in only his third full season of racing. Began racing in 1969 on a BSA Gold Star, but broke a shoulder and a hand at Croft in only his fourth meeting. Moved south from Yorkshire, and won the Lord of Lydden title on his 750 cc Dunstall Norton. Joined the Gus Kuhn Norton team, and won the £2,000 Mellano Trophy at the 1972 Hutchinson 100, and his first British title.

Cal Rayborn

BORN 1940. Long time Harley-Davidson factory rider, and regarded as America's top road racer. Holder of the world's motorcycle land speed record at 265.49 mph on a 1,480 cc V-twin Harley. Winner of the Daytona 200 in 1968 and '69. Sensation of the 1972 Anglo-American match races when, in his British debut, he won three of the six races. Winner of the 1972 Indianapolis and Laguna Seca AMA nationals.

Phil Read

BORN 1939. Won the Senior Manx Grand Prix in 1960. The next year, he won the Junior TT on a Bill Lacey Norton in his TT debut. He joined Yamaha in 1963, won four world titles as a Yamaha factory rider, and also claimed the 1971 250 cc world title on his privately owned Yamaha. Has won a total of six TTs. In 1972 he rode the John Player Nortons and joined racing's most famous team, MV. Scored his first win for MV in the 350 class of the 1972 East German GP.

Tony Rutter

BORN 1941. First raced in 1962 on a 350 cc BSA Gold Star at Brands Hatch, and is now one of Britain's leading short circuit riders. The 1971 British 350 cc champion on the Yamaha of sponsor Bob Priest, he joined the John Player Norton team in 1972, but left after an unhappy spell. Bounced back to finish second to Agostini in the 1972 Junior TT, recording his first 100 mph Isle of Man lap at 100.9 mph.

Jarno Saarinen

BORN 1946. A former ice racing champion of Finland, he switched to road racing to become his country's first motorcycling champion. Finished fourth in the 1970 250 cc world championships, after missing rounds to take a degree in mechanical engineering. Second in the 350 series in 1971 and third in the 250 series, he finally clinched the 250 title in 1972. A Yamaha works rider, he has always refused to race at the TT, which he considers too dangerous. Winner of the 1972 Race of the Year at Mallory Park.

Barry Sheene

BORN London 1950. Son of well-known rider and entrant Frank Sheene. Made his racing debut as recently as 1968, and was quickly being tipped as a future world champion. Almost fulfilled these forecasts in 1971, when he finished second in the 125 cc world championship on his privately owned Suzuki twin. Won 125 British championship in 1970 and '71. Joined Yamaha's factory team in February 1972, but a complicated shoulder injury marred his GP season that year. Brother-in-law of equally famous Paul Smart.

Paul Smart

BORN 1943. Started racing in 1965 after a period as a self-confessed 'ton-up kid'. First major success: 1970 Bol d'Or 24-hour race, with Tom Dickie as co-rider on the works Triumph. A member of the winning British team in the first Anglo-American match races in 1971, he later left BSA-Triumph to join Bob Hansen's Kawasaki team in America. Winner of the two richest races in 1972—the Imola 200, on a works V-twin Ducati, and the Ontario Champion Spark Plug Classic, on a Seeley Kawasaki.

Percy Tait

BORN 1929. The grand old man of British road racing (but don't mention age to him), Tait has been riding for more than 20 years. Despite competition from riders half his age, he had the drive and experience to win the MCN Superbike series, the 750 cc British championship, the Bol d'Or 24-hour race (with Ray Pickrell) and the Thruxton 500-miler (with Dave Croxford), all in 1971. A Triumph rider almost all his life, latterly on the 750 cc three-cylinder thoroughbreds.

Chris Vincent

BORN 1935. The undisputed king of British sidecar racers. Began road racing in 1959 after winning the 1958 British sidecar grass track championship. Seven times British champion, and holder of the sidecar lap record at almost every British circuit at one time or another. Winner of the 1962 500 cc sidecar TT, he switched to the four-cylinder Munch outfit in 1972 after many years of racing his own BSAs. At the Finnish GP in 1972 he became the first British sidecar rider in eight years to win a world championship race. Also an accomplished solo racer and speedway sidecar rider.

Peter Williams

BORN 1939. Son of famous AMC race engineer Jack Williams, he led the John Player Norton team in 1972. Started racing in 1963 on a 350 cc Manx Norton at the late age of 24. British 500 cc champion in 1970. A brilliant TT rider, he has finished second six times on the Isle of Man, but has still to win his first TT. Gave the John Player team their first major victory, in the 1972 Hutchinson 100.

Results of major F750 and F750-type races since 1969

FORMULA 750, the class for 750 cc machines based on production engine components, was launched in America in 1969 and is now the most popular in road racing. This appendix gives results of most F750 races run since 1969. Also included are races not run to strict F750 rules, but in which F750 machinery has competed. They are listed here because they played an important part in the development of F750 machines. Races run to full F750 rules are marked with an asterisk.

1969

Daytona 200*
1 Cal Rayborn (750 Harley-Davidson)
2 Ron Grant (500 Suzuki)
3 Mike Duff (350 Yamaha)

Race of the Year
1 Giacomo Agostini (500 MV)
2 Ken Redfern (750 Norton)
3 Dave Croxford (750 Kuhn Commando)

Race of the South
1 Giacomo Agostini (500 MV)
2 Mick Andrew (750 Kuhn Commando)
3 Phil Read (350 Yamaha)

1970

Daytona 200*
1 Dick Mann (750 Honda)
2 Gene Romero (750 Triumph)
3 Don Castro (750 Triumph)

Race of the Year
1 John Cooper (350 Yamsel)
2 Phil Read (250 Yamaha)
3 Paul Smart (750 Triumph)

Race of the South
1 Giacomo Agostini (500 MV)
2 John Cooper (350 Yamsel)
3 Phil Read (350 Yamaha)

Race of the South F750*
1 Paul Smart (750 Triumph)
2 Ray Pickrell (750 Triumph)
3 Percy Tait (750 Triumph)

1971

AMA races

Daytona 200*
1 Dick Mann (750 BSA)
2 Gene Romero (750 Triumph)
3 Don Emde (750 BSA)

Atlanta 125-miler*
1 Kel Carruthers (350 Yamaha)
2 Dick Mann (750 BSA)
3 Ralph White (500 Kawasaki)

Loudon 100-miler*
1 Mark Brelsford (750 Harley-Davidson)
2 Kel Carruthers (350 Yamaha)
3 Dick Mann (750 BSA)

Kent 100-miler*
1 Dick Mann (750 BSA)
2 Kel Carruthers (350 Yamaha)
3 Don Emde (750 BSA)

Pocono 100-miler*
1 Dick Mann (750 BSA)
2 Kel Carruthers (350 Yamaha)
3 Yvon Du Hamel (500 Kawasaki)

Talladega 200*
1 Yvon Du Hamel (500 Kawasaki)
2 Dick Mann (750 BSA)
3 Don Emde (750 BSA)

Ontario 250-miler*
1 John Cooper (750 BSA)
2 Kel Carruthers (350 Yamaha)
3 Ron Grant (500 Suzuki)

Motor Cycle News
Superbike Championship

Brands Hatch
1 Percy Tait (750 Triumph)
2 Charlie Sanby (750 Kuhn Commando)
3 Martyn Ashwood (700 Weslake Metisse)

Mallory Park
1 Percy Tait (750 Triumph)
2 Ray Pickrell (750 BSA)
3 Peter Williams (750 Norton)

Snetterton
1 Percy Tait (750 Triumph)
2 Ray Pickrell (750 BSA)
3 Charlie Sanby (750 Kuhn Commando)

Oulton Park
1 Ray Pickrell (750 BSA)
2 Percy Tait (750 Triumph)
3 Dave Nixon (750 Boyer Trident

Mallory Park
1 Ray Pickrell (750 BSA)
2 Percy Tait (750 Triumph)
3 Ken Redfern (750 KJ Dunstall)

Brands Hatch
1 John Cooper (750 BSA)
2 Ray Pickrell (750 BSA)
3 Percy Tait (750 Triumph)

Superbike Championship Table

1 Percy Tait (750 Triumph) 99 pts
2 Ray Pickrell (750 BSA) 93 pts
3 Charlie Sanby (750 Kuhn Commando) 40 pts

Other British events

Thruxton 200-miler*
1 Ray Pickrell (750 BSA)
2 Paul Smart (750 Triumph)
3 Dudley Robinson (350 Yamaha)

F750 TT*
1 Tony Jefferies (750 Triumph)
2 Ray Pickrell (750 BSA)
3 Peter Williams (750 Norton)

Silverstone
1 Paul Smart (750 Triumph)
2 Percy Tait (750 Triumph)
3 Ray Pickrell (750 BSA)

Race of the Year
1 John Cooper (750 BSA)
2 Giacomo Agostini (500 MV)
3 Ray Pickrell (750 BSA)

Race of the South
1 John Cooper (750 BSA)
2 Giacomo Agostini (500 MV)
3 Ray Pickrell (750 BSA)

750 cc British Championships

1 Percy Tait (750 Triumph) 60 pts
2 Charlie Sanby (750 Kuhn Commando) 49 pts
3 Tony Jefferies (750 Triumph) 35 pts

1972

AMA events

Daytona 200*
1 Don Emde (350 Yamaha)
2 Ray Hempstead (350 Yamaha)
3 Dave Smith (350 Yamaha)

Atlanta 125-miler*
1 Yvon Du Hamel (750 Kawasaki)
2 Paul Smart (750 Kawasaki)
3 Gene Romero (750 Triumph)

Loudon 100-miler*
1 Gary Fisher (350 Yamaha)
2 Mark Brelsford (750 Harley-Davidson)
3 Gene Romero (750 Triumph)

Indianapolis 125-miler*
1 Cal Rayborn (750 Harley-Davidson)
2 Yvon Du Hamel (750 Kawasaki)
3 Gene Romero (750 Triumph)

Laguna Seca 125-miler*
1 Cal Rayborn (750 Harley-Davidson)
2 Gene Romero (750 Triumph)
3 Paul Smart (750 Seeley Kawasaki)

Talladega 200*
1 Yvon Du Hamel (750 Kawasaki)
2 Gary Nixon (750 Kawasaki)
3 Art Baumann (750 Suzuki)

Ontario 250-miler*
1 Paul Smart (750 Seeley Kawasaki)
2 Geoff Perry (750 Suzuki)
3 Renzo Pasolini (750 Harley-Davidson)

John Player Transatlantic Trophy

Brands Hatch, race 1
1 Ray Pickrell (750 Triumph)
2 Cal Rayborn (750 Harley-Davidson)
3 Phil Read (750 John Player Norton)

Brands Hatch, race 2
1 Cal Rayborn (750 Harley-Davidson)
2 Ray Pickrell (750 Triumph)
3 Peter Williams (750 John Player Norton)

Mallory Park, race 1
1 Ray Pickrell (750 Triumph)
2 Cal Rayborn (750 Harley-Davidson)
3 John Cooper (750 BSA)

Mallory Park, race 2
1 Cal Rayborn (750 Harley-Davidson)
2 Ray Pickrell (750 Triumph)
3 John Cooper (750 BSA)

Oulton Park, race 1
1 Cal Rayborn (750 Harley-Davidson)
2 Ray Pickrell (750 Triumph)
3 John Cooper (750 BSA)

Oulton Park, race 2
1 Ray Pickrell (750 Triumph)
2 Cal Rayborn (750 Harley-Davidson)
3 John Cooper (750 BSA)

Continental events

Imola 200
1 Paul Smart (750 Ducati)
2 Bruno Spaggiari (750 Ducati)
3 Walter Villa (750 Triumph)

Swedish GP*
1 Kent Andersson (350 Yamaha)
2 Phil Read (750 John Player Norton)
3 Tony Jefferies (750 Triumph)

Motor Cycle News
Superbike Championship

Brands Hatch
1 Ray Pickrell (750 Triumph)
2 Peter Williams (750 John Player Norton)
3 Phil Read (750 John Player Norton)

Cadwell Park
1 John Cooper (750 BSA)
2 Tony Jefferies (750 Triumph)
3 Ray Pickrell (750 Triumph)

Brands Hatch
1 Ray Pickrell (750 Triumph)
2 John Cooper (750 BSA)
3 Peter Williams (750 John Player Norton)

Mallory Park
1 John Cooper (750 BSA)
2 Ray Pickrell (750 Triumph)
3 Ken Redfern (750 BSA)

Oulton Park
1 Paul Smart (750 Triumph)
2 Ray Pickrell (750 Triumph)
3 John Cooper (750 Triumph)

Scarborough
1 Mick Grant (750 John Player Norton)
2 Dave Croxford (750 Seeley BSA)
3 Ray Pickrell (750 Triumph)

Mallory Park
1 Paul Smart (750 Seeley Kawasaki)
2 Yvon Du Hamel (750 Kawasaki)
3 John Cooper (750 Triumph)

Brands Hatch
1 John Cooper (750 Triumph)
2 Phil Read (750 John Player Norton)
3 Peter Williams (750 John Player Norton)

Superbike Championship Table

1 John Cooper (750 Triumph) 112 pts
2 Ray Pickrell (750 Triumph) 84 pts
3 Peter Williams (750 John Player Norton) 57 pts

Other British events

F750 TT*
1 Ray Pickrell (750 Triumph)
2 Tony Jefferies (750 Triumph)
3 Jack Findlay (750 Suzuki)

F750 race Hutchinson 100*
1 Paul Smart (750 Ducati)
2 Phil Read (750 John Player Norton)
3 Tony Jefferies (750 Triumph)

F750 race Silverstone*
1 Percy Tait (750 Triumph)
2 John Cooper (750 Triumph)
3 Tony Jefferies (750 Triumph)

Race of the Year
1 Jarno Saarinen (350 Yamaha)
2 Paul Smart (750 Seeley Kawasaki)
3 John Cooper (750 Triumph)

Race of the South
1 Phil Read (750 John Player Norton)
2 Paul Smart (750 Seeley Kawasaki)
3 Peter Williams (750 John Player Norton)

750 cc British Championships

1 Dave Potter (750 Kuhn Norton) 64 pts
2 Brian Adams (700 Weslake Triumph) 53 pts
3 Darryl Pendlebury (700 Weslake Triumph) 38 pts

APPENDIX 3

Where to go

A guide to Britain's racing circuits

THIS SECTION is a guide to the permanent circuits in Britain which regularly stage motor-cycle road racing. It gives an outline map of each circuit and a map showing the approach roads to the venue. There are also helpful details of where to apply for tickets, the track length, the exact geographical location, how to attend by public transport and the type of racing presented.

Brands Hatch

Address:
Brands Hatch Circuit Ltd, Fawkham, Near Dartford, Kent.

Telephone:
Ash Green 872331.

Location:
20 miles south-east of London on A20, near Farningham.

Length:
Grand Prix circuit, 2.65 miles; Club circuit, 1.24 miles.

How to get there:
Bus—Greenline 719 from London to Wrotham. For local services telephone Swanley 2075.
Train—from Victoria, Holborn Viaduct, Sevenoaks and south coast to Swanley. Special bus service from Swanley station for major meetings.

Used for:
International, National, and Club racing.

Cadwell Park

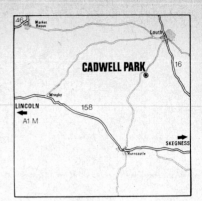

Address:
Chas Wilkinson, Cadwell Manor, Louth, Lincs.

Telephone:
Louth 3779/Stenigot 248/651.

Location:
7 miles north-west of Horncastle on A153, 5 miles south-west of Louth.

Length of circuit:
2.25 miles; club circuit, 1.5 miles.

How to get there:
Bus—services from Lincoln and Sleaford to Horncastle. From Grimsby, Market Rasen and Lincoln to Louth.

Used for:
International, National and Club racing; also moto cross.

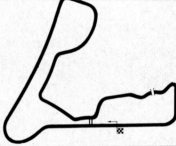

Castle Combe

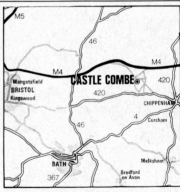

Address:
Castle Combe Circuit, Chippenham, Wilts.

Telephone:
Castle Combe 278; Castle Combe 395 (race and practice days only.)

Location:
5 miles north-west of Chippenham on B4039.

Length of circuit:
1.84 miles.

How to get there:
Bus—399 service from Bristol to Chippenham. Train—Chippenham station on Paddington to Bristol line. Timetable enquiries Chippenham 2252.

Used for:
National and Club race meetings.

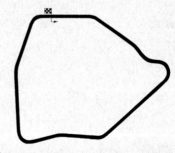

Croft Autodrome

Address:
Croft Autodrome, Croft, Darlington, Co Durham

Telephone:
Croft 206/659.

Location:
7 miles south of Darlington, 5 miles east of Scotch Corner.

Length of circuit:
1.75 miles.

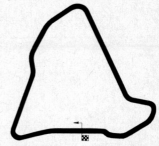

How to get there:
Bus—service from Darlington station to circuit. (Weekdays and Bank Holidays 12.23, Sundays 13.15.)
Train—Darlington station from Kings Cross.

Used for:
National and club racing.

Darley Moor

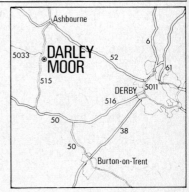

Address:
Darley Moor Circuit, A515, Ashbourne, Derbyshire.

Telephone:
Rugeley 2563.

Location:
Four miles west of Ashbourne, on A515.

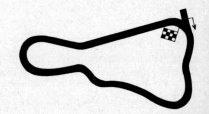

Length of circuit:
1.5 miles.

How to get there:
Bus services from Ashbourne.

Used for:
Club racing.

Lydden

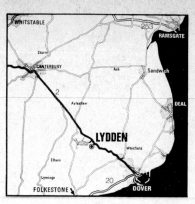

Address:
William Mark Holdings Ltd, 71 West Street, Sittingbourne, Kent.

Telephone:
Sittingbourne 72926; Shepherdswell 557 (race days only).

Location:
7 miles south-east of Canterbury, Kent.

Length of circuit:
1 mile.

How to get there:
Bus—East Kent Line service 15 from Canterbury. Hourly service.
Train—Shepherdswell on Southern Region Victoria to Dover.

Used for:
National and club racing; also speedtrack racing and moto cross.

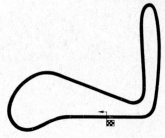

Mallory Park

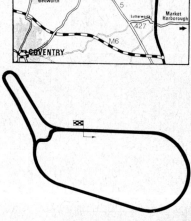

Address:
Mallory Park, Kirkby Mallory, Leics.

Telephone:
Earl Shilton 2631.

Location:
9 miles south-west of Leicester just off A47.

Length of circuit:
Long circuit 1.35 miles; Club circuit 1 mile.

How to get there:
Bus—688 service from Hinckley to Kirkby Mallory. 658 service from Leicester to Earl Shilton.
Train—Leicester station. Timetable enquiries to Leicester 29811.

Used for:
International, National and Club racing.

116

Oulton Park

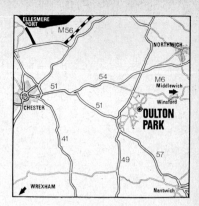

Address:
Cheshire Car Circuit Ltd, Oulton Park, Little Budworth, Tarporley, Cheshire.

Telephone:
Little Budworth 301.

Location:
Near Tarporley off A54.

Length of circuit:
2.76 miles.

How to get there:
Bus—North Western Road Car Co services from Manchester, Macclesfield, Warrington and Altrincham to Northwich, then shuttle service to circuit from bus station. Timetable enquiries to Stockport 2213.
Train—Crewe station. Timetable enquiries to Crewe 55123.

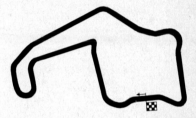

Used for:
International, National and Club racing.

Scarborough

Address:
Scarborough Racing Circuits, 17 Pavilion Square, Scarborough, Yorkshire.

Telephone:
Scarborough 64341.

Location:
Close to Scarborough town centre.

Length of circuit:
2.4 miles.

How to get there:
Ten minutes' walk from Scarborough town centre.
Train—Scarborough station from Kings Cross.

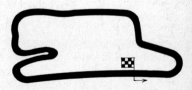

Used for:
National and International racing.

Silloth

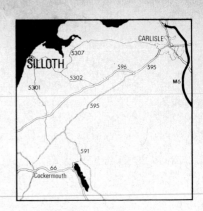

Address:
Solway Motor Cycle Racing Club, 14 Barras Close, Dalston, Carlisle, Cumberland.

Telephone:
Carlisle 23422 (extension 359) day; Dalston 710654 night.

Location:
12 miles west of junction 41 on M6 on the west Cumberland coast.

Length of circuit:
1.1 miles.

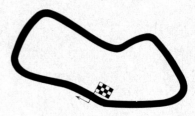

How to get there:
Bus—services from Whitehaven and Carlisle.
Train—Carlisle station from Euston.

Used for:
Club racing.

Silverstone

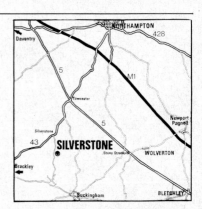

Address:
Silverstone Circuit Ltd, Silverstone, Near Towcester, Northants, NN12 8TN.

Telephone:
Silverstone 271.

Location:
15 miles south-west of Northampton on A43.

Length of circuit:
Grand Prix circuit 2.927 miles, Club circuit 1.608 miles.

How to get there:
Bus—345 service from Northampton bus station to Silverstone village.
Train—Northampton station from Euston.

Used for:
International, National and Club racing.

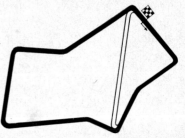

Snetterton

Address:
Snetterton Circuit Ltd, Snetterton, Norwich, NOR 1OX.

Telephone:
Quidenham 303/4.

Location:
10 miles north-east of Thetford, Norfolk on A11.

Length of circuit:
2.71 miles.

How to get there:
Bus—12 service from Norwich to Attleborough. Timetable enquiries to Norwich 20491.
Train—Attleborough and Thetford stations on Norwich to Cambridge line. Timetable enquiries to Norwich 20255.

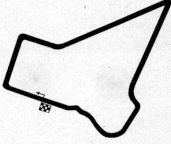

Used for:
International, National and Club racing.

Thruxton

Address:
Thruxton (BARC) Ltd, Thruxton Circuit, near Andover, Hants.

Telephone:
Weyhill 344.

Location:
4 miles west of Andover, on A303.

Length of circuit:
2.356 miles.

How to get there:
Bus—Apply to Wilts & Dorset Motor Services Ltd, Bridge Street, Andover (Andover 2339).
Train—Southern Region stations to Andover. Connecting coach service arranged for major meetings.
Coach—Royal Blue Express Coach Services, National House, Queen Street, Exeter (Exeter 74191).

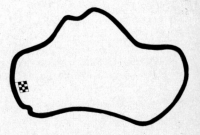

Used for:
International, National and Club racing.

Useful trade addresses

Racing motorcycle manufacturers, importers and specialists

AGRATI SALES (UK) LTD
St Mark's Street,
Nottingham
(Nottingham 50616)
(Kawasaki importers)

BSA MOTOR CYCLES LTD
Armoury Road,
Birmingham 11
(021-772 2381)

VIC CAMP MOTOR CYCLES
131 Queens Road,
Walthamstow,
London E17
(01-520 2093)
(Ducati importers)

H DUGDALE MOTORS
Greenbank Garage,
Alvanley,
via Warrington,
Cheshire
(Helsby 2692/2417)
(Yamaha racing specialists)

BRYAN GOSS MOTOR CYCLES
Vincent Street,
Yeovil
Somerset
(Yeovil 21681)
(Maico importers)

LAWTON AND WILSON
264 Millbrook Road,
Southampton
(Southampton 27744)
(Italian Harley-Davidson importers)

NORTON VILLIERS EUROPE LTD
North Way,
Andover,
Hants
(Andover 61414)

PADGETT BROS
44-46 Wellington Street,
Batley,
Yorks
(Batley 4968)
(Yamaha racing specialists)

COLIN SEELEY RACING DEVELOPMENTS LTD
Stapley Road,
Belvedere,
Kent
(Erith 36817)

SUZUKI (GB) LTD
87 Beddington Lane,
Croydon CRO 4TD
(01-684 9456)

JOHN TICKLE (RACING EQUIPMENT) LTD
Cromwell Road,
St Neots,
Hunts
(St Neots 73281)

TRIUMPH ENGINEERING CO LTD
Meriden Works,
Allesley,
Coventry
(Coventry 20221)

WESLAKE AND CO LTD
Harbour Road,
Rye, Sussex
(Rye 3062)

Components and services

AMAL LTD
Holdford Road,
Witton,
Birmingham 6
(021-356 4801)

J. W. E. BANKS AND SONS LTD
Crowland,
Peterborough PE6 0JP
(Crowland 316)
(Koni dampers)

CASTROL LTD
Burmah-Castrol House,
Marylebone Road,
London NW1 5AA
(01-486 4455)

CHAMPION SPARKING PLUG CO LTD
Feltham,
Middlesex
(01-759 6442)

DUNLOP RUBBER CO LTD
Fort Dunlop,
Erdington
Birmingham 24
(021-373 2121)

FERODO LTD
Chapel-en-le-Frith,
Stockport,
Cheshire
(Chapel 2520)

GIRLING LTD
Kings Road,
Tyseley,
Birmingham 11
(021-706 3371)

JOSEPH LUCAS LTD
Great King Street,
Birmingham 19
(021-554 5252)

R. T. QUAIFE ENG LTD
Botany Industrial Estate,
Vale Road,
Tonbridge,
Kent
(Tonbridge 3747)

RENOLD LTD
45 Northwood Street,
Birmingham 3
(021-236 4114)

LESTER SIMMS
12 Burwell Road,
London E10 7QG
(01-556 6805/6)
(NGK spark plugs)

Racing schools

DIXON RACING LTD
35 Wodeland Avenue,
Guildford,
Surrey
(Guildford 66635)

KIRBY CAMP RACING SCHOOL
131 Queens Road,
Walthamstow,
London E17
(01-520 2093)